The Music of India

EARLY 17TH CENTURY PORTRAIT OF BHAWANI DAS
A PAKHWAJ PLAYER
From Messrs. Luzac & Co.'s Collection

Frontispiece

The Music of India

Atiya Begum Fyzee-Rahamin

WITH ILLUSTRATIONS

LOW PRICE PUBLICATIONS
Delhi-110052

First Published 1925
Reproduced 1990, 1994

FYZEE, RAHAMIN, ATIYA BEGUM
ISBN 81-85557-94-2

Published by :
LOW PRICE PUBLICATIONS [A Division of D.K. Publishers Distributors (P) Ltd.
at Regd. Off. A-6, NIMRI Community Centre Ashok Vihar, Phase-IV,
Delhi-110052]

Printed at :
Raj Offset Printers, Delhi.

PRINTED IN INDIA

FOREWORD

It was in a tiny fishing village near the seaside, Bombay, in 1913. The spring had donned its garment of green splendour, and the spreading beauty of the world without saturated with waves of golden light the feathery swaying palms ; the sun shining on an indulgent ocean, lapping the palm-fringed silvery beach. The nightingales had burst into a flood of song. The murmur of waves, the breezes, the humming of the bees, beat in unison, creating a continual music.

Emotions were roused. It was a call of the ancient exquisite beloved Art. I sang the eternal limpid melodies. Rahamin immortalized them in a series of beautiful paintings, the *Rāgas* and *Rāginis* (the male and female melodies). I dashed off a few lines in explanation. We soon left for Europe, where the written text was brought out in book form, and helped to explain the symbolic significance of the *Rāgas* and *Rāginis*.

The leading motive of Indian music is an expression of the feelings and emotions in a series of melodies ; these being woven with the legends and traditions of the poetic fancies and reveries of the human soul and spirit of the country. Long ago these sounds reached far and wide, growing more lovely as appreciation increased. Then they grew fainter and fainter, diminishing gradually through the past century and a half, till they finally passed away, leaving strange discordant noises and tumultuous shouts, foreshadowing oblivion.

However, our never-tiring efforts have proved somewhat successful, and the past five or six years point to the break of the dawn in the musical world of India. Three conferences have been held, and Pandit V. N. Bhatkhande's forty years' study of ancient manuscripts and experiences, his magnetic personality, his remarkable patience and sweet temper, gained the confidence and respect of all the *Ustaads* (practical experts) from whom he extracted a store of melodies and created his own *Lakshan Geet* (musical compositions), systematically set them to notation in a series of works invaluable to students, but they are not yet complete. Music will once more sound the never-ending melancholy, wisdom and renunciation of the East.

I have to thank the Thakur Śri Jessrājsinghji Seesodia of Udaipur for reading the manuscript and for the footnotes and appendix, also for correcting the proof sheets.

It is hoped to follow this work by another volume, giving minute details and classification of the different melodies set to notation, with charts and diagrams.

ATIYA BEGUM FYZEE-RAHAMIN.

CONTENTS

CHAPTER I

Works on Indian Music

Few subjects have been more enveloped in mystery and darkness than Indian music. After careful research we find that there is no dearth of material on the subject, and that, from the region of fancy and fable of thirty or forty centuries ago, attempts, during long intervals, have been made to collect, rearrange, assimilate and consolidate existing practices, so as to reduce the same to an intelligible and workable system. But, for lack of interest by Indians, this rich harvest of their ancient literature now lies buried in dusty manuscripts, and unless superhuman exertions are directed towards its recovery, our knowledge of this science must remain defective and unconnected.

Indian music is so very ancient that it would not be exaggeration to credit its origin to the primitive gods.* To trace something of its history the old Sanskrit literature must be divided into four periods, according to modern European method of calculation : the *Mantra* period, from 2,000 to 1,500 B.C. ; the *Chhand* period, from 1,000 to 800 B.C. ; the *Brāhmana* period from 800 to 600 B.C., and the *Sûtra* period, from 600 to 200 B.C. This takes us back to a time which, though it may seem lost in the mists of antiquity, clearly shows that in all these ages music not only existed but had attained a very high degree of perfection, and that the musical scale, the fundamental basis of the science, and the result of musical activities of ages past was practised by the *Vedic Rishis*.

The Aryans were, therefore, foremost in bringing the art of music to a very high standard, development and creative genius were the fruit of the ages.

The *Sāma-Veda* (hymns), extracted from the *Rig-Veda*, to be chanted during the sacrifices, have their own metrical system. The rules for chanting

* It is a Hindu tradition to attribute all ancient Hindu works to mythological personages.

and singing the *Vedas* are laid down in the *Sāma Sutras*, and possess all the fine elements of our present music, with a proper musical notation to denote the metre and the mode of chanting.

"Let an *Udgātri** (priest *Sāma* singer) who is about to perform the sacrificial work desire that his voice may be sweet in tone and let him acquire the musical notes with *Udgītha* (sound pure and simple), and by that *Udgītha* which has acquired musical notes, perform the rites of the *Rit-Vij*," so says authority.

The *Sāma Vedāchchala* was a *Sāma Sûtra*, a treatise of seven chapters, denoting the method of singing the *Vedas*, directing the modulations, intonations, trills, etc., of letters, syllables and tones ; music being shown to be co-relative with the teaching of the *Vedas* and an inseparable part of devotion. The hymns of the *Vedas* were sung ; *Upavedas* developed it as an art and the *Rishis* and *Munis* included it in their studies.

The *Gāndharva Veda* is justly looked upon with Divine reverence. When and by whom it was composed is shrouded in mystery, though almost all the ancient works of music have wholly and solely drawn upon the *Gāndharva Veda*, when dealing with its technicalities.

There are traces, dim and obscure, that even previous to the compilation of the *Gāndharva* and *Sāma Vedas*, a free and original spirit of long duration was at work in the domain of music. That there was a succeeding age of a still greater length in which that spirit was condemned is proved from the *Dharma Shastras* of the *Rishis*.

Now the *Vedic* period established music as an art. The *Brāhmana* period shows that not only was the musical scale practised by the ancient *Aryans*, but its internal value to notes was studied scientifically. This would be unintelligible without the admission of a preceding musical age.

The *Upanishad* literature of the *Brāhmana* period is closely enveloped by the mystical symbolism which characterized ecclesiastical Hinduism of that age. But when the verses are stripped of their spiritually enigmatical garb they are connected with the corresponding number and value of notes, *Murchanās*, *Grāma*, etc., of music and their subtle compositions treat of the numbers indicating their relation to musical scale and its intervals. They

* Called also a *Sāmagah*.

had songs which differed from hymns and the names of the metric hymns and songs were associated with the names of gods.

"Let me sing for the immortality of the gods, for desires of mankind, for securing grass and water for ailment, for self and for Heaven to the institutions of sacrifices." "The vowels constitute the body of *Indra*, the sibilants and '*ha*' that of *Prajāpati*, and the consonants that of *Death*." "Should anyone revile the singer about the sibilants and '*ha*,' he should say: I seek the protection of *Prajāpati*, who will grind thee down"; and about the consonants: I seek the protection of *Death*, who will hurl thee into flames.

The vowels are to be recited with sound and force, saying: I seek the strength of *Indra*.

The sibilants and "*ha*" are to be sounded internally, yet distinctly, saying: To *Prajāpati* I resign my life.

The consonants are to be repeated slowly and distinctly, saying: From *Death* I extricate myself.

The singer was then revered and protected from any ridicule.

In the *Chhāndogya* and other *Upanishads*, in spite of the strong tendency to mystify everything, it says, that: "In chanting the *Vedas*, the deeply significant and supernatural '*Om*' is articulated." What is "*Om*"? It is the All-Pervading, All-Essential, All-Absorbing; the All-Sacred.

Rik is the essence of speech, *Sāma* is the *Prān* (breath). *Rik* and *Sāma* make a *Maithuna* (couple). *Udgītha* is *Svara* (sound, pure and simple), and *Udgītha* is the quintessence of all essences.

"Om" is *Udgītha*, the most supreme and most adorable of all. It is listened to in the ether of the human heart with its seven sounds, which, having settled in the soundless supreme, unmanifested *Brāhmana*, become undistinguished and indistinguishable as the various flavours of the flowers are lost in the honey, securing safety and immortality.

Thus the *Udgītha* and its epitomized sound "*Om*," is a composition of music and notes with words.

The *Shīkshā* (phonetics) were compiled by the sage, *Yajñavalkya*, a *Rishi* of the *Brāhmana* period, and the recognized author of the *Sukla* (bright) *Yajur Vedas*. He mentions the *Anusthuba* (a metre), which was practised with considerable acquaintance of its intrinsic value and ratio, and refers to it as having existed in the *Gāndharva Veda* in his *Shīkshā*. This exquisite *Anusthuba* was used in the *Vedic* period for a passage in the *Rig Veda*, which runs thus : " Poets by their wisdom discovered *Indra* dancing to the *Anusthuba*."

Yajnavalkya, in explaining the so-called *Atman* (self) to his wife *Maitriya*, quotes a verse which not only classifies the deities, the castes, of the *Rishis* and metres into three divisions under the appellation of *Uchca*, *Nicha* and *Svarīta*, but groups the seven notes *ri* with *dha*, *ga* with *ni*, and *sa* with *pa* and *ma*, in such a way that it points to the extremely advanced form of the progress by fifths, technically.

Pingala Sūtras were written by *Pingalānga*. In the *Sutra* period he was the greatest authority on *Chhandas* (metres).

Next we come to the popular *Bhagvad Gīta*, which is so favourably disposed to music and treats it affectionately and comprehensively, unlike the *Anugīta*, a later portion attached to the *Bhagvad Gīta*, which discloses a forward form of Hindu thought, but condemns music altogether, similarly as do the law-givers *Manu*, *Apasthamba*, and others in the *Dharma-Shāstras*. This emphatic condemnation of *Sangīt* (dancing, singing and playing) showed that it was a separate art altogether, and that it had reached a high state of perfection and was all-absorbing.

The *Gīta*, in securing to itself almost all the oldest, highest and best religious and secular matters of the early Hindu institutions, gives preference to the *Sāma* among the *Vedas*, to the *Gāyatri* among the *Chhandas* (metres), to *Chitraratha* among the *Gāndharvas* (ideal celestial choristers), and to *Nārada* among the *Rishis*.

In the Buddhist period, all the writings and teachings speak of music, musical instruments, songs and dances as a part of existence. Musical references are continually given in dialogues on high moral principles to be adopted in life.

Amarsinha was the celebrated Buddhist compiler of a lexicon, called after his own name Amar Kosha, in which the seven notes are treated at length.

The *Mrichchakatikā*, or the Toy Cart, was a work of considerable importance written by *Kumbhālika*, in the reign of King *Śudraka*, about the time of Christ, giving the number of diatonic scales in describing the flute and *vina*.

In the fifth century *Kālidāsa* brought the musical executions in his drama possibly to render it suitable to the heroine who was a *Gandharva*. Singing, dancing and gesticulating were intimately connected with dramatic representations, and the classic writers in introducing them in the Sanskrit dramas were undoubtedly fully acquainted with the chief features of the art of music.

The *Nātya Shastra*, by *Bharata*, is a commentary on the drama and therefore treats more of acting; except in the three or four chapters which throw most useful light on the allied arts. He says: "The poet, who is always the musician in India, is to employ choice and harmonious expressions and an elevated and polished style embellished with the ornaments of rhetoric and rhyme."

From the seventh to the nineteenth centuries there is a veritable library of works on the subject. It is praiseworthy that, in the absence of settled homes and peaceful kingdoms, the *Pandits* devoted their lives to making imperishable records, connecting the link of prehistoric music to the ensuing centuries. After the Muslim invasion, *Rāgtarangini** was among the first most important work written by *Lochanakavi* in the twelfth century.

Sangīt Ratnākar† was another book written by *Sārangadeva* in the thirteenth century. It ranks as one of the premier authorities on singing and dancing, yet, in spite of *Kalināth's* great commentary on the *Sangit* in 1425, it faded into insignificance and became almost unintelligible within a hundred and fifty years of its production.

The four Sanskrit works: *Nartananirnaya*, *Rāgāmala*, *Rāgamanjarī* and *Sadrāgachandrodaya*, by *Pundarīka Vittala*, are invaluable for the store of knowledge and information they possess.

Rāgavibodha‡ was produced by *Somanāth* in the year 1610. *Sangīt Darpana* was a popular work composed by *Dāmodara Misra* in 1625. *Sangīta Parijāta* was brought out by *Ahobala Pandit* a little later. The excellence of this last-named work can never be extolled enough.

The three *Granthas Anupalvilāsa*, *Anupankusha* and *Anupatatnāra*, by *Bhāvabhatta*, were written at the end of the 17th century.

* *Rāgtarangini*, by Lochanakavi, is about the sixteenth century.

† *Sangit-Ratnākar* of Sarangdeva has many other commentaries besides *Kalināth*, such as *Khumbhkarnedra* Tikà, *Sinhabhūpāla* Tika and others.

‡ The *Rāgavibodha* is one of the most important works on music in Sanskrit, as it is a complete exposition of classical Hindu music, written in a clear and easy style.

The dramatic compositions of *Sudraka*, *Kālidāsa* and *Bhavabhuti* are immortal by their extraordinary beauty. Such an abundant, varied and rich treasure of poetic genius has never been brought to play upon the emotions and finer sentiments of any other people. They are arrayed in metrical form so as to be sung with musical rhythm and performed with proper gesticulations.

In the eighteenth and nineteenth centuries, when the remnants of the Mohamadan power were struggling to hold the sceptre in *Ajodhya* (Oudh), three works were produced worth mentioning. *Naghmaé Asafī* was written by *Mohamad Raza*. Here, for the first time, we come across a reliable authority with the *Bilāval* scale as the *Shuddha* scale, a scale which is the foundation of Hindustani music. At the same time, *Maharaja Pratap Singh Deva*, of *Jaipur*, in an outburst of musical enthusiasm, collected all the experts together and with their help brought out a book called "*Sangīta Sāra*," and to him was attributed the authorship owing to his great patronage.

Sangīt Kalpadruma was the last important *Grantha* (book) of the nineteenth century, by *Krishnananda Vyas*.

The whole of the 19th century shows a gap under Western influence, and the last ten years however, once more point to a musical outburst, the perfect work of late *Sahebzāda Nawāb Saadat Ali Khan* of *Rampur in Urdu*, on music, was unfortunately left unfinished owing to his sudden death.

Thakur Nawab Ali Khan of Akbarpur has collected nearly 300 *Dhrupads* and *Haris* of the House of Rampur in his work in Urdu, *Maarifat e Neghamāt*, published recently.

Pandit V. N. Bhatkhande has written some very important works on music in Sanskrit, and is still collecting most of the famous songs from *Ustaads* and setting them to notation ; this contribution of his to Indian music will be of great service.

CHAPTER II

Practical Experts

A large quantity of Hindu classical music must remain sealed to us, for we do not at present possess the means to reach and collect the *Granthas* secreted in the different private libraries of India. Small gleanings from the scattered fragments dispersed through works on theology, mythology and literature show that ancient Hindu music abounds in artistic, philosophic and scientific speculations.

Of the various arts and sciences in which the cultured Aryans indulged, the art of music occupied their chief attention.

Nārada, the *Vedic Rishi*, the distinguished son of *Barhmā*, was a musician of exquisite skill. His invention of the wonderous *Vīna* is thus described in the poems of *Māgha*: Nārada sat watching his large *Vīna* which, by the impulse of the breezes, yielded notes that pierced the regions of his ears successively, preceded by musical intervals.

Tambur was a *Rishi*, prior to *Nārada*. The *Tambura* used by the beggars and ascetics derived its name from him ; and from thence comes the English " tambourine."

Jayadeva composed hymns and set them to music 1000 B.C., or 1000 years A.D., according to two counter versions.

Bharata was the first inspired sage who invented dramatic representations and they consisted of three kinds, *Nattya*, *Nritya* and *Nritta*.

Shiva, the Divine Dancer, added two other styles : the *Tāndava* and *Lasya*. *Lasya* was taught to Prince *Wisha* by *Shiva's* wife, the *Goddess Parvati*. The Prince instructed the *Gopies* of *Dwarka*, and from them it was communicated to the women of *Saurashtra*, from whom, in turn, it passed to the women of different regions.

Ravana was a proficient performer and allotted a large part of his province to the maintenance of experts. There is a musical instrument, played in *Gujerat*, called after his name, *Ravanhatta*.

The kings were patrons and artists of music and it formed a part of the early education of Princes ; even the royal ladies cultivated *Sangīt* (dancing, singing and gesticulating), in their own *Sangīt Shālas* (music salons), built specially for that purpose, and attached to their palaces.

Chand* remarks of this : " The *Chohan* was past master in the art, both vocal and instrumental."

Abstemious Buddhists and recluse Jains, too, were not indifferent to the charms of music. *Gautama Buddha*, the noblest and greatest religious reformer the world has ever seen, was deeply versed in music, and expounded his doctrines by musical representations and references.

Ashva Ghosa, who travelled with a party of musicians about the beginning of the Christian era, was the means of converting many persons of distinction by the skill and magic of his performance. In his " Life of Buddha," he says : " They placed the dead body of *Tathagatha*, using all kinds of dances and music." He also says : " To win over the deity is to sing its praises and prayers." Music hath power to make the Heavens descend upon earth, and displays the early innate belief in the mythical portrayal of this wonderful science.

The *Gāndharva Veda* (art of music) was destined to exercise a world-wide influence in later years. A methodical system of notation had already been worked out before the age of *Panini*, the great grammarian, who lived about 600 B.C., and very much later this was drawn upon by the Persians, Greeks and Arabs, and lastly by Europeans.

Behram Gor, Emperor of Persia, hearing of the marvels of Hindu musicians, invited them ; and the enormous number of 10,000 *Lurians* (musicians of common type), who were sent by King *Shankol* of *Hind*, were encouraged by his munificence to enter his domain. The dancing girls in Persia were called *Kasuli*, a corruption of *Kabuli*.

When the celebrated Greek harpist, Terpander, introduced A and E and Pythagoras B, completing the diatonic scale, in the sixth or seventh century before Christ, the Hindus had already established a complete diatonic scale

* Chand or *Chand Bardai*, the Court Bard of *Prithivirāj Chohān*, the last great Hindu Emperor of Delhi.

in India. It was Alexander who carried the chromatic scale from the banks of the Indus to his country, the Greeks being the only historical nation of the ancient world who had adopted the *Murchana* (quarter tone).

Hindu music, the origin of all music, thus crept into Persia, then to Greece, and onward to Arabia, from-whence it was again brought to India, blending itself once more into the parent stock and forming the modern Hindustani music.

With the advent of the Muslims, about a thousand years ago, all Hindu thought was marred and checked; but eventually the stranger not only adopted Hindu music as an ennobling art, but, by powerful and forcible patronage and intercourse, changed somewhat the feature of the original music. The South of India being less disturbed by foreign intervention and bloody warfare, retained the material of Aryan emotions and feelings, and preserved the *Shastric* traditions. So that it is safe index to what music was, in its early stages. It is accurate and therefore capable of being studied with the help of regular text books. The northern became duly confused and disconnected, dividing music into the two present systems: the *Hindustani* or northern, and the *Karnātaki* or southern. These two schools have existed in the country for several centuries and the chief difference lies in their two perfectly independent *Shuddha*, or primary scales. The *Hindustani* is based on the *Bilawal* scale and the *Karnātaki* on the *Kanakāngi* scale.

Of the two kinds, the alluring fascinations, graceful embellishments, and pleasing excellencies of the northern, even in its present completely degenerate state, cannot possibly be denied.

Music has existed in Arabia since prehistoric times. At the crossing of the Red Sea. Moses and the Children of Israel sang a hymn of thanksgiving; and Miriam, the prophetess, Aaron's sister, played on the *Duff* (tambourine) and danced with all her women.

David played divinely on his *Kanoon* (harp), his chanting being known as *Lahné-Daodi*. His *Kanoon* was of considerable size, and had seventy-five strings. This was the origin of the spinet, which ultimately led to the pianoforte.

Singing girls and poets sang in assemblies and entertained the listeners. With the advent of Islam women still sang and played.

The singer who acquired great fame after the foundation of Islam, was *Towais of Medina*, a slave of Osman, son of Affan.

Caliph Omar (634) was a composer.

Caliph Osman (644) was a patron of the great musician *Ibne Surreid*.

Caliph Ali (656) and *Caliph Moawiya* (661) were great patrons of music and freely cultivated the art.

Yazid (680) was a composer.

In 687, when *Abu Zobair* was rebuilding the *Kaaba*, he employed masons from Syria and Persia, and they sweetened their labours by singing the songs of their country.

In the eighth century, music had become a necessary adjunct to Arab life.

Walid I (705) was a performer on the lute.

Caliph Abu Abbas (749) and *Mansur* (754) were great patrons of music, whilst *Mehdi* (775) was not himself a marvellous musician, but all his children were accomplished in the art.

Ibn Musjah, a negro slave, listened with rapturous longing, and to acquire efficiency repaired to Syria, where Greek and Roman sciences were imparted, and in further quest travelled to Persia, completed his studies and returned to his country a finished performer.

Baghdad had now become the capital of the Arab empire, which stretched from Tartary in the East to Spain in the West. Here were gathered all the finest musical talent in all Arabia. It was the golden age of Arabian music. Here was held the refined and dazzling court of the son of *Mehdi*, the world-famous *Caliph Haroun Al Rashid* (786), whose name is immortal in Eastern song and story. The unlimited patronage of art and music at his court is on the lips of the Arab minstrel to-day. Schools and colleges set apart for music sprang up throughout the empire.

About 780 A.D., the poet *Khalil* had written his "Book of Sounds" and "Book of Rhythm." Another writer of that period was *Obeidulla Bin Abdulla*, who wrote a treatise on the "Tones and Mutations in Song." Then came *Al Kindi*, who, in 862 A.D., wrote six books on music : (1) On composition ; (2) Laws of tones ; (3) Elements of music ; (4) Book of rhythm ; (5) On instruments ; (6) Union of poetry and music. His pupil, *Ahmad Bin Mohammed*, wrote works on music, including an introduction to the science of music.

Then there were the practical and professional musicians, who were famed throughout the length and breadth of Arabia. The first of these was the great *Ibrahim of Moussil* (742-803), called the patriarch of Arabian music. *Junis Suleeman*, and *Zobair Ibn Dahman*, who was such a favourite at the court that two villages were assigned to him as a reward for his musical gifts.

Mabed of Medina, who introduced female singers in the harem.

Mohammed Ibnal Hares, who wrote a book on singing.

Abu Aisha, son of Motawakil, was a composer of 300 songs.

Isaak (767-849), son of Ibraham, no less renowned than his father, was the author, composer and editor of many important works.

Among the famous singers of Arabia were *Oriel*, great poetess and composer, who boasted of knowing 21,000 melodies by heart; *El Garid* and *Ibn Soreid Schuma*, the rival singers at court; *Selsel*, who died 791; *Jelid-Ibnal*, whom Haroun had commissioned, with two others, to collect the songs written during his reign; and *Mokarek*, who flourished in 800-864.

At Cordova, the capital of Arab Spain, the cultivation of the arts and sciences was carried out on a greater scale than at Baghdad. In the reign of *Caliph Hakam I* (796), a famous Baghdad musician named *Sarjab* was invited to the court of Cordova. He was a pupil of the celebrated *Ibrahim of Mossoul*. He arrived in Spain in 821, and under the Caliph's patronage opened the music school of Cordova, which afterwards became famous for its musicians and theorists. Other music schools were opened at Seville, Granada, Valencia and Toledo.

The field of Arabian music growing extensive, tens of thousands of tunes were composed. Expressed opinion and critical examinations of the art led to the compilation of a large number of books. The most famous work was that of the renowned and learned *Abul Farah* (died 918), of Ispahan, entitled *Aghani*, in twenty-one large volumes! The aim of this stupendous record, ten centuries ago, was to illustrate the one hundred select tunes of the *Abbasid* period, explaining their nature and scope, and tracing their origin. These melodies were based upon an elaborate scale system, called the *Messel* system. They had seventeen notes in the scale. All the melodies were derived from the twelve principal scales, or modes, called the *Makamats*.

(1) *Rahavi* was sung from early dawn till sunrise.

(2) *Hoosseini* till three hours after sunrise.
(3) *Iraki* till noon.
(4) *Rasta* at midday.
(5) *Koochick* three hours before sunset.
(6) *Busalik* at a little after noon.
(7) *Ushhak* near sunset.
(8) *Jangla* for three hours after sunset.
(9) *Buzurag* follows *Jangla*.
(10) *Nava* at midnight.
(11) *Ispahani* follows *Nava*.
(12) *Hijaz* comes last.

Six other modes were called: *Schenas*, *Meia*, *Selmek*, *Noores*, *Khardamiah* and *Koucht* respectively.

The nature of these scales was demonstrated by circles divided into eighteen points, representing the seventeen tones, and from these "circulation of modes" resulted the eighty-four scales, showing a very accomplished and complete system.

Serjal, a known genius, had introduced a less complicated but thoroughly finished system of his own in all his music schools in the ninth century.

Other names include: *Ben Zeidan*, *Rabbi Enock*, *Rabbi Moses*, *Vadel*, *Moheb*, *Abil*, *Mousali*, the pupil of *Serjab*, and *Abu Bekr Ibn Bajeh*, of Granada, who wrote a commentary on Aristotle's "Treatise on Sound," and whose songs were very popular. Then we have *Abdul Mounini* (eleventh century), *Mohammed bin Ahmadel Haddah* (twelfth century), and *Mohammed Shirazi* (thirteenth century). There has been no dearth of musical theorists, and in the fourteenth century all arts and sciences were put forth with considerable vigour, and music specially had quite a revival. The leader of this revival was an Arab of Baghdad, named *Safiuddeen Abdel Monim*, whose principal work, the *Schereffige*, was written in the Arabic tongue; the works of *Mohammed Ben Abu Bekr*, *Ben Scerouni*, and *Abdul Khader*, must also be mentioned.

Thus the Greek and Persian element, based on ancient Hindu music, found its way into the heart of the desert Arab, and pouring out its impressive tones, caught the vast empire of the Caliphs from Sindh to Spain.

Laya and *Tāla* (rhythm and time) had also reached high perfection. Seventeen varieties of *Tāla* were in use. It was this music, the original old Hindu music metamorphosed, that was brought back by the Muslim settlers into India. More than twelve centuries ago, when the Arabs first entered Sindh they found the temples of Multan thronged by women votaries, the sacred seats of Muttra, Benares, Ajodhya, Northern India, and the famous temples in Gujerat and Deccan, crowded by artists. Singing and dancing was very freely indulged in, under the patronage of religion. Arab musicians settled in Sindh and gradually came in contact with Hindu music, with the result that the real blending and fusion of the two systems of music began in the eleventh century, which is the birth of Hindustani music. There were many musicians in the court of *Mahmood Ghaznavi*, but they sang Persian songs. *Avicenna*, a contemporary of Sultan Mahmood, was the last great Muslim author of a book on music.

The taste for pure Indian music was produced by the *Sufis*, whose religious tendencies inclined towards devotional demonstrations and made them extremely popular both with Hindus and Muslims. They came originally from Baghdad and introduced the Dervish's ecstatic dance.

In the reign of Sultan Altamash, the leading exponent, Kazi Hamidudin of Nagor, got admission to the Royal Court and the *Sufi Chisties* gave religious sanction. This tended towards popularizing *Sufi* music at once and people began to indulge in it unrestrainedly. The intermixing continued with vigour and *Sangīt Ratnakar* was brought out in the reign of Sultan Feroz Shah, son of Altamash, in 1237, and adds a valuable link to the music of that period. By this time the music with the foreign element was sung in all Courts by both sexes.

Sultan Alauddin, the founder of the Khilji Dynasty, was a great lover of music, and the cultivation of music grew to high perfection under his Royal patronage. The number of the Court experts was unlimited. *Changi*, *Fatuha*, *Nasir Khan*, *Bahroz*, all flourished in his reign. The romantic Persian poet and court musician, *Amir Khusru*, has left a permanent mark by inventing the *Kavāli* style of singing, and several *Ragas* (tunes), like *Zeelaf*, *Sarparda*, *Sazgiri*, etc. are attributed to him. His mixed composition in *Brij-Bhasha* and Persian are of intoxicating beauty and sweetness. He is also the inventor of *Tarana* singing and the musical instrument *Seh-tar* (three wires), generally mis-called *Sitar*.

The Deccan was the seat of music in those days, and when the Sultan conquered it, he took hundreds of male and female performers to the North, among them being the great *Naik Gopal*, of unrivalled fame. The latter was presented at the royal court and his defeat in musical combat with the exclusive genius, *Khusru*, was an event of great importance.

Deccan was flooded by great masters of this art, and the city of *Vijayanagar* was the principal magnet which drew hundreds into its ocean of melodic lustre, under the patronage of its great Hindu emperors. At every gate of the city wall hundreds of dancing girls were stationed. Demonstrations were given by them on every occasion and they led the royal processions and danced in durbars.

In the reign of *Sultan Mohamad Tughluq* a circular structure called *Tārābād* was erected in *Dowlatābād*. This was embellished with tastefully furnished apartments all round, and a great hall in the centre. In these elegant rooms, open to view, reclined beautiful maidens, on swings, surrounded by hand-maids in glittering costumes. The *Darogha*, or leader, was a Persian nobleman of high extraction, named *Shamsuddin Tabriz*.

The title of *Amir* was bestowed on the preceptor, thus pointing to the prestige and status in which music was held in those days. This " elysium of joy " was reserved for the entertainment of royal guests, who, as a great mark of favour, were located there. A variety of performances took place, under the able guidance of the *Chodhary*, in the domed hall reserved for the purpose.

The harmony of Arab-Persian-Hindu music had by this time resulted in such tunes as *Zeeluf*, *Nowroz*, *Zangulla*, *Iraq*, *Yemen*, *Husaini*, *Zilla*, *Durbari*, *Hijāz*, *Khamaj*, etc. These were adopted and sung all throughout the Empire.

In the illustrious reign of the dazzling *Timorias*, a still more vigorous impulse was given to all arts and reforms ; hence there are endless elegant mementoes of a brave, noble, brilliant race, who conquered, governed, achieved everlasting glory, and then passed away. *Tan-Sen*, the unapproachable, still inspires one with awe, standing high like a luminous star of unabated brilliance, scintillating throughout the confused centuries.

Raja Man Tanwar, the ruler of *Gwalior*, invented the *Dhrupad* style of singing, and the school of *Gwalior* rose into prominence.

Sultan Hoosein Sharki of Jaunpur was another devoted lover of music. *Naik Bakshoo*, whose powers were second to none ; *Baijoo*, *Pandvi*, *Lohung*, *Jurjoo*, *Bhagwan*, *Dhondee* and *Daloo*, were all renowned musicians of those times.

The *Ain-i-Akbari* speaks of thirty-eight most efficient musicians attached to the Royal Durbar, in the reign of the mighty Emperor Akbar, who was a great reformer, a patron of all arts and sciences, and a great lover of music.

Haridas Swambi, Tan-sen's Guru, was a musician and sage, who lived at Brindaban on the sacred banks of the Jumna. The *Swami's* seraphic compositions form the basis of many legendary records.

The *Rajput*, *Rani Mirabai of Udaipur*, poetess-musician, dissatisfied with the vanities of the world, consecrated her life to the services of *Bhajans* (divine compositions) in the temple at *Chitor*. This beautiful monument stands to-day known as Mirabai's temple. The wind whistles a mournful melody to the invisible spirit that may still haunt its beloved precincts.

The dulcet pathos of *Surdās*, *Kabirdās*, *Bhikodās*, *Tulsidās*, *Hardās*, *Lada-Kapola*, their predecessors and successors, are remembered and cited with affection and reverence to this day. These were godly men, who preferred asceticism to worldly enjoyment and made music their life-long study. The eminent *Pundarik Vittal*, too, lived in these glorious times.

In *Akbar's* glorious reign the fountains of learning overflowed and spread to all parts of the vast Empire.

Tān-Sen, the divinely inspired, unequalled paragon of cadences, personification of sound, was one of the *Nau-Ratan* (nine gems) of the illustrious royal court. He was India's last brilliant jewel in the sphere of music, the hero of countless legendary stories, and now lies buried in a modest grave in *Gwalior*. His tomb is overshadowed by a tamarind tree. Musicians make, pilgrimage to his memory, lay offerings at the tomb, and a strong superstition prevails that by chewing the leaf of that tamarind tree, the human voice gains in sweetness and beauty. The descendants of *Tān-Sen* are now known as *Senyas*, and mostly inhabit the district of Alwar.

The famous singers of *Jehangir's* Court were *Chatar Khan*, *Parvizād*,

Jehangirdād, *Khurramdād*, *Makhu*, *Hamzān* and *Bilās Khan*, son of *Tān-Sen*.

The principal artists of *Shah Jehan's* durbar were *Jagannāth*, who received the title ot *Kavirāj* (prince of poets) from the Emperor, *Dirang Khan*, *Lal Khan*, known as *Gunsamudra* (ocean of excellences), and the son-in-law of *Bilās Khan*. *Dirang Khan* and *Jagannāth* were awarded their weight in silver in token of appreciation. *Jagannāth* was probably the father of *Bhavbhatta*.

In the latter half of the eighteenth century, Muslim power declined and the country began to be influenced by the English, and the decay of all indigenous arts set in. A slow and sure death gripped the cult of music too.

Mohammad Shah, *Rangilay** (coloured), 1719 A.D. was the last Emperor who had performers of repute attached to his Court. Among them were *Adarang*, *Sadrang*, the inventors of the *Khyal* style of singing, and *Shori*, the initiator of the *Tappa* style of singing. Most of their compositions are associated with the name of *Mohammad Shah*. They brought these stvles to the highest form of perfection. Enticing, classical adornments were the feature of many new modes, like *Rekhta*, *Quol*, *Terana*, *Tervat*, *Guzzal*, *Kulbana*, *Marcia*, *Soz*, etc. *Noor khan*, *Ladoo-khan*, *Piyarekhan*, *Janee*, *Goolam Rasul*, *Shakoor*, *Mukhan*, *Tethoo*, *Methoo*, *Mohammad Khan* and *Chejjoo Khan* were all experts of fame.

Since the advent of the Muslims, theoretical labour was reserved to the Hindu authors and Sanscrit scholars, and vocal exercise was practised by the Muslims, lately in blissful ignorance of theory. *Naghmāt* was written in the time of *Asafuddowlah*,† who was an expert musician.

The Kings of Oudh were the last rulers holding the sceptre of Muslim supremacy in India, and all the members of the royal family excelled in the art of dancing and singing. The last king, *Vajid Ali Shah* was a past master in the art.

The classical music of India seemed to be coming to an end.

The followers of *Tān-Sen* were divided into two musical sections, the

* *Rangilay* literally means the coloured, but the sense of it is "the merry." We do not know how far poor Mohammad Shah was merry as his reign was one long internal and external conflict the Sayid King-makers created all the internal troubles, the *Marathas* under the great Baji Rau and the Persians under Nadir Shah kept him quite merry the whole of his long reign.

† The *Vazir-Navab* of Lucknow.

Rubābiyas and *Beenkars*. Both schools are represented to-day in *Rampur*, a state sheltered by an amphitheatre of the Himalayan range, in the north of India : the *Rubābiyas* are represented by *Mohamad Ali Khan* and the *Beenkars* by *Vazir Khan*, the descendant of *Nabi Khan* of the court of Emperor *Mohamed Shah*.

The rulers of *Rampur* have not only been great patrons of ancient art but were themselves celebrated musicians and poets. *Nawab Kalbe Ali Khan* and *Shah Zadeh Saadat Ali Khan* were both musical geniuses ; while *Nawab Hamid Ali Khan*, the present ruler, combines the great tradition of his royal house. He is the most perfect and charming embodiment of a poet-musician. All that is left of the three arts of old India, dancing, instrumental playing, and singing, is now centred in *Rampur* and represented by a group of extremely clever practical experts. Hidden from the curious gaze of man's eye are *Vazir Khan Beenkar*, *Piyare Saheb Drupadiya*, *Musta Khan Khayali*, *Ali Raza Khan*, singer of *Kaul Kalbana* and *Fida Husein*, the *Sarode* player. *Muhamad Ali Khan*, *Rubab* player, *Achchan*, the wonderful dancer of the house of *Kalka Binda*, is also included. All these excel in their own sphere and are complete masters in their respective art.

They have disciples in whom they are endeavouring to keep alive the noble legacies handed down to them from their forefathers.

Rampur guards its knowledge and musical culture with such jealous care that very few are privileged to enjoy the sweet strains in full. Guests are honoured with an occasional performance, but the greater wealth and love of it remains with those who are versed in it.

In these benighted days of modernism in India meagre attempts to revive music are made ; some from ancestral pride, and others from artistic spirit ; and in spite of their very slight knowledge of the subject they have succeeded in producing music of pliability and sweetness, and with a command of voice that still has the power to enthrall audiences.

Among the many strivers, the names of *Mohammad Khan*, *Serhoobai*, *Omraokhan*, *Khoshal Khan*, may be mentioned. *Haddoo Khan* held an undisputed sway over his contemporary *Khyal* singers, so did *Hasoo Khan* and *Tanras Khan*. *Vazir Khan* (*Dhamar* singer) ; *Alijan*, *Tassudduck*, *Rasul* and *Dewji* (*Tirwata* and *Tarana* singers) ; *Babu Jotsinghji*, *Kudao Singh*, *Jorawar*

Singh, *Nasrat Khan* (*Pakhawjis* or drummers) ; *Gookam Ali* (*Sarode*-player) ; *Varis Ali*, *Jamaluddin Khan*, *Musharaf Khan* (*Been* players) ; *Bahadur Sen Khan* (*Rubab* player) ; *Imrat Sen*, *Rahim Sen*, *Kale Khan* (*Gobarhari Dhrupadias*); *Ali Hussein*, *Zakiruddin Khan* (*Khandari Bani Dhrupadias*) : all the fore-mentioned, some now dead, did or are doing much to maintain the past glories of northern music, groping in the dark to grasp the hidden meanings, in vain sacrificing their lives to attain the unknown, the "breathing tragedies" of confused humanity.

Thus we see that at a very early period of history, Indian music had developed into a science rich and perfect in composition, combining in a high degree the requisite virtues of melody and symphony.

With Muslim influence northern music underwent vital changes, gaining considerably in beauty. With the decline of Muslim power the art of music declined. During the early supremacy of the English, the remaining vitality was completely crippled. They thought it semi-barbarous. One or two scholars, Sir William Jones and Ralph Griffiths, made some attempts to understand the subject, but their interest was academic and antiquarian. At present, music receives no support or impetus from the Government whatsoever, with the consequence that it has deteriorated both in quality and quantity. Had it not been that music came to be more or less confined to the Durbars, it would have been totally extinct. These Court-artists were preserved and exhibited more as curiosities than as exponents of a great art. Even the Indian princes under the so-called "new education," acquired hybrid notions and began to display indifference towards Indian music. The older generation of musicians died away without bequeathing their knowledge to their representatives and descendants.

The last hundred years point to the fact that under the unsympathetic atmosphere of the Westerners no literature of any status was created nor were there any practical experts of great repute. All that remained of a once superb art lay buried in the dusty mists of deplorable neglect. Such a state of medley consequently resulted in producing upstarts and charlatans, who, affecting poses, had the impudence to bring out books on the subject, also speaking to a sensation-loving public in the western world and India, a matter completely meaningless and misleading.

1 The late Abraham Pandither of Tanjore (*Sruti Expert*)
2 The late Khansaheb Zakiruddin Khan of Udaipur
3 Atiya Begum Fyzee-Rahamin
4 Pandit V. N. Bhatkhande of Bombay

Facing page 26.

It is therefore with a deep-felt feeling of gratitude and satisfaction that in the absence of all congeniality, we find that a few men have sacrificed their precious lives in the study of this beautiful science and crowned their most noble efforts in bringing to light what was till very recently engulfed in the darkness of fabulous lore. Among the limited number of selfless scholars, *Brahma Sri Bhatkhande* of Bombay, the authority on Hindustani music, has embodied the results of his great labours in a publication, entitled "*Lakshya-Sangitum.*" It has come at a time all too significant in the era of music. He has recapitulated all the most important points of the historical survey of Hindustani music and reconstructed a workable system on a sound *Shastric* foundation, embracing the music of the north and south. No one but a creative genius like *Brahma Sri Bhatkhande* could have brought about such a completely harmonious blending of the two kinds of music.

This was originally written in simple Sanskrit, and to make it accessible in his Presidency, he wrote a copious commentary on it in *Marathi*, of which three volumes, exceeding fifteen hundred pages, have already appeared; attempts are being made to translate it into *Gujerati*. *Thakore Nawab Ali Khan* of Akbarpur, Oudh, has put it in *Urdu* under the name of *Mārifat-i-Neghmāt* for the *Urdu* reading public of the north. He is an able musician and a contemporary of *Brahma Sri Bhatkhande*.

This is the first step of vital importance towards the regeneration and revival of Indian music, and *Brahma Sri Bhatkhande* has placed the entire musical world under a deep obligation.

Popularizing and cultivating the science as an art or vice-versa, imparting its true essentials for mass education, all that constructive and practical work remains to be done.

CHAPTER III

History of Indian Music

Indian music is three thousand years old. It is considered to be of Divine origin. It is by far the most complicated and intricate system of music among the musical systems of all nations, and a science hardly to be excelled by any creation of the human mind.

It has a highly-coloured and fascinating history to be found in the ancient texts, preserved and handed down to us, surviving cycles of ages and the ravages of time.

Like all old branches of learning, it is based upon the religious faiths, observances, legends and traditions of the country, depicting the social manners and customs of the people, in the history of the tunes and words of the song. There are various versions as to the origin of Indian music. The traditions most often quoted are: (*a*) That it is descended from *Brahmā*, brought into vogue by *Mahadev* and *Nārada*, and performed by the great *Naiks* (i.e. Masters of Music) from time to time. (*b*) That a strange bird called *Musikar* or *Dīpak-Lata** inhabited the Caucasus mountains, and its beak had seven apertures; through each of these openings he was able to blow a different note, and at different seasons of the year he combined these notes into harmony and produced *Rāgas* † congenial to that particular hour of the day and season of the year. His age was a thousand years and when death drew near he fell into a state of ecstasy, and accumulated a pile of combustibles from his environs, and

* Dīpak—literally means fire, it is also the name of a *Rāga*, male tune in Indian music. The peculiarity of this wonderful tune is that when it is played with the right notes in the right season, its power is so great that it excites the element of fire in nature, and creates fire.

Lata—means hot scorching winds.

† Rāga means tune; there are six *Rāgas*, i.e., male tunes in Indian music, and each *Rāga* has its own five or six *Rāginis*. These tunes have seasons of the year and hours of the day, when they should be played or sung. Any departure from the rigid law lessens the beauties and subtleties of the tunes and violates the sanctity of the art.

danced around it in a state of absolute frenzy, playing the various notes and tunes from his beak for a length of time, in harmony with the seasons. When, however, he touched upon the notes of the *Rāg Dīpak*, fire was at once ignited, the pile burnt up, and ultimately he himself plunged into it, and became *Sati*.

After a time an egg was created out of the warm ashes which in due course became a *Dīpak-Lata*.

Thus from times immemorial, one bird was born, lived its weird life and in the end turned to ashes ; then another and another. The bird is supposed to be extinct now.

This is the strange and fanciful story, handed down to posterity, and which every musician of repute is fond of repeating.

From the earliest times, we find that music was regarded as sacred. It sprang from God and was performed by the smaller divinities. There were professional celestial beings, such as the *Gāndharvas* and *Apsarās*, who performed before the *Devās*.

Brahma indulged in the art for relaxation. *Saraswati*, the goddess of learning and music, invented the exquisite *Vīna*, which bears her name. *Nārada* is a brilliant figure among the divine beings, in the musical world. *Shiva*, in the act of dancing his divine dance, shook the universe with his marvellous performance. His wife, *Pārvati*, has been the subject of many a poetical idea. The *Rudra Vīna* is the definite representation of her lovely sleeping form.

When the art was cultivated so freely among the *Devās* in Heaven, it affected the mortal beings on earth. The kings indulged in it, so did their subjects, until the study of music was considered to be of vital importance in ancient times. It was a compulsory subject of education. The youths were taught to sing the divine praises and prayers. And the secular studies were imparted to them in tunes.

Thousands of musicians of all grades flourished in the land, and multitudes of professionals were supported by the State, free from all impositions ; their one object in life was to unravel the secret mysteries, and expound the hidden doctrines of the sacred art.

There were no religious rites, ceremonials, forms and observances, inside or outside a home, in which music did not play an important part. The very existence of the people seemed to depend upon its practice.

Temples and shrines, and all sacred places, were thronged with devotees, who were all absorbed in that class of music called "Devotional Music," night and day.

The villages had bards and minstrels who entertained the village folks with tales of the miraculous deeds of the *Devās*; philosophies of the ascetics and sages; biographies of noble and highly placed men and women, and love romances in tuneful verses. As time went on, India passed through many vicissitudes and changes. People were thrown into a chronic state of disturbance. Their pet vocations were interfered with, and they were more or less deprived of their freedom of living.

But the present degradation and neglect of music show the remarkable degeneration and low status to which Indians have sunk. All the creative genius of which the land was so rich, is effectually crushed out, until no trace of its former glory is left.

To acquire anything of Indian music, in the present day, one has to be specially gifted by the gods. We have no facilities for learning, in the way of preliminary books or notations, nor have we any recognized schools of high order or merit, accessible to the lover or seeker of music. All the mysteries of this sublime art are confined to the ancient literature in unintelligible *Brij-Bhasha* or intricate *Sanskrit*, carefully hidden away from the gaze of the masses, in some remote corner.

Music was handed down traditionally in certain families celebrated as great artists, and almost all the male members among them were able to play and sing, and during a certain period of Indian history you heard of great men, like *Naik Gopal*, *Naik Baijoo Tān-Sen*, *Amir Khusru*, *Mir Nasir Ahmad Dehlavi*, etc., springing up from the unknown, and stirring the very forces of nature by their extraordinary performances.

These families are still to be found; they are few and far between, and scattered in the north and south of India. They have knowledge of these priceless texts, and some are even in their possession, but they guard these with religious care.

At the present day, the craze for the revival of old arts has resulted in a few musical schools, scattered in Bombay, Baroda, Mysore and Calcutta, in which the self-styled professors have brought out a number of school series, called "Notations," imitating the Western system of setting music to notation. The harmonium has been introduced in place of the sweet strains of *Sarangi* (Indian violin) for accompanying purposes.

A more disastrous metamorphosis cannot be imagined. There is not the slightest idea or semblance of the rich, classical and original Indian melodies, in these chopped-out, hybrid, silly tunes, sung by a number of students together.

Similarly some tunes of modern invention are set to music and played in the band. They are anything but Indian in character. As a matter of fact, the real Indian music is so constituted that it does not lend itself to such roads to popularity as the piano-organ, school choruses, bands, theatre orchestras, etc.

It is much too sacred, beautiful, almost divine for light amusement, and a thorough knowledge of it requires self-abnegation and the serious study of a life-time.

MATH*

A peculiar feature of Indian music is the distressing and confusing institution of *Maths*, i.e., the classification of *Rāgas* (male tunes) and *Rāginīs* (female tunes) and *Tālás* (time).

From the ancient *Rāgmālas* and *Sangīts* (works on music) we find that music was regarded with awe and reverence. The *devās* indulged in it, and men of great learning and piety, such as those who had submerged their individualities in the divine path.

Sixteen thousand tunes and three hundred and sixty *Tālás* (times) are mentioned as used by them in those days, almost inconceivable to our minds and understanding.

The divine *Krishna* was entirely intoxicated by his own music on the flute, and when he commenced to sing, his sixteen thousand *Gopis* followed him, each producing a *Rāga*.

In the Middle Ages it was brought to a comparatively appreciable and

* The word *Math* means opinion ; but here it means the various schools into which Hindu music is divided.

systematic basis, overshadowing the inaccessible heights of the so-far sublime music.

Four *Maths* were decided upon, each named after the divinity who was the originator of it.

(1) Someshvar or *Shiva Math*. *Someshvar* is one of the appellations of *Mahadev* (Adam).

Math literally means intelligence. This *Math* is named after *Mahadev*, and the method of singing and playing in this *Math* is like the method with which *Mahadev* sang and played, and one which is extremely difficult.

It has six *Rāgas* and thirty *Rāginīs*. Each *Rāga* having its own six *Rāginīs* and eight *Putrās* (sons).

(2) Kalināth Math—so named after *Krishna*, who was once playing with a ball on the banks of the sacred *Jumna*, with his playmates. In the enthusiasm of a throw the ball fell into the river, *Krishna* immediately jumped in the water in search of it. When he reached the bed of the river he found himself perched on one of the thousand heads of a monster serpent. The king of serpents inhabited the *Jumna*. The King Serpent on being thus ruthlessly disturbed was annoyed and tried to injure him with the head on which he stood.

Krishna jumped gracefully on to another head, and thus by jumping on to different heads avoided its deadly bites, till at last he found a piece of rope with which he successfully tied the serpent up, and thus freed himself from danger.

Now this feat of springing from one head to another was done with such infinite grace and beauty that it caused a peculiarly pretty dance, with elegant actions and movements, which the historians are pleased to comment upon, and this to-day is a recognized form of dancing.

Now when he got hold of the string and mastered the situation, he began to sing in sheer joy ; he sang with a certain method, and this method was called *Kālinath Math* commemorating that incident. Like *Someshvar Math*, *Kālinath Math* has also six *Rāgas*, and each *Rāga* has its own six *Rāginīs* and eight *Putrās*.

(3) Bharat Math, so called after the great *Bharat Muni*, who sang religious songs called *Bhajans*, in praise of the *Devās*, in an easy facile manner—creating

a certain mode of singing and playing, distinguishing it from the two others in method of execution and arrangement of tunes.

This *Math* has six *Rāgas*, and each *Rāga* has its own five *Rāginīs*, and eight *Putrās* and eight *Bhāryās* (daughters-in-law) of the *Putrās*.

This is the only *Math* which has the additional *Bhāryās*.

(4) Hanuman or *Hanou Math*, so called after the famous general of *Sri Ram Chandraji*. *Hanuman*, the king of monkeys,* who conquered *Lanka* (Ceylon), and flushed with victory in the noted battle, sang praises in the Court of *Sri Ram Chandrji*, after a certain style.

This style was recognized ever since and one which is very much in vogue in Benares to-day.

Similarly to *Bharat Math*, this *Math* has six *Rāgas*, and each *Rāga* has its own five *Rāginīs* and eight *Putrās*. The *Bhāryās* of *Bharat Math* are retained in this.

The last two *Maths* are very much akin to each other in the seasons of the year when they should be played or sung, also the arrangement of the tunes, with a slight variation here and there.

These *Maths* show an enormous modification in tunes and times. They were brought to a standard of one's reach and understanding.

The sixteen thousand tunes were reduced to six *Rāgas* and thirty or thirty-six *Rāginīs*, each *Rāga* having its own five or six *Rāginīs*, according to their individual *Math*, and eight *Putrās* and eight *Bhāryās*, and the three hundred and sixty *Tālas* were reduced to ninety-two *Tālas*.

Each *Math* played the tunes in a certain order which it recognized ; for instance, one *Math* qualified a tune with a certain attribute, with one or two notes *Tīvar* (sharp) or *Kōmal* (flat), and classed it among the *Rāginīs*, while another *Math* with a similar alteration ranked it among the *Putrās*, and so forth.

This difference of opinion caused an incessant wrangle, never determining the class of the tune, but raising an interminable field for enquiry and research in this branch.

In the reign of the Emperor *Akbar*, the court musician *Tān-Sen* made a thoroughly arduous and minute study of this superb science ; felt the super-

* **The word " monkeys " is used here instead of " aborigines," owing to a misconception of the mediæval commentators of the epic poem *Rāmayana*, as the aborigines of South India being uncivilized at the time of *Rāma's* invasion of *Lankā*, were called *Vānaras*, really meaning " forest men " (*Vana-Nara*) has come to be considered " monkeys."**

fluity of the four *Maths*, and after long observation, determined the distinctive qualifications and characteristics of each melody, and revolutionized the musical world of India by deciding upon one *Math* only, with its proper order of tunes. He dealt similarly with the *Tālas*, and concentrated the ninety-two *Tālas* into twelve, without lessening the significance, beauty and subtlety of each tune and time.

None but a master-mind like that of *Tān-Sen* could have brought about such a complete upheaval in so intricate an art.

He is supposed to have written a *Rāga-Māla* (book on music) on a sound systematic basis, and ascribed it to his own name.

This tended to make music intensely popular and progressive. This is the *Math* which has been followed more or less since, and has greatly influenced modern northern Indian music.

In the south of India music is of an entirely different character, the instruments also differ a good deal from the north. They have a system of their own. Instead of classifying the tunes according to *Maths* and having so many *Rāgas* and *Rāginīs*, they simply have seventy-two *Rāgas*, otherwise scales. And each scale has a name which signifies the notes of which it is composed. They follow the ancient system of music of *Narada* and have their own history and traditions.

CHAPTER IV

Sapt-Prakarna

Every Indian science is divided into its various component parts, these are called *Angās* in Sanscrit, which means (limbs) parts. Music in India is hence divided into *Saptānga** or seven parts, which are as follows :

(1) Sur-Adhaya—the part which treats of tones including semi-tones, demi-semi tones, etc.

(2) Tāl-Adhaya—the part which treats of time or rhythm.

(3) Rāg-Adhaya—the part which treats of tunes or melodies.

(4) Ast-Adhaya—the part which treats of musical instruments, such as *Vina*, *Sitar*, *Ta-oos*, *Nafiri*, *Bānsri*, *Sankh*, etc., played either by the hand or mouth.

(5) Nirt-Adhaya—the part which treats of dancing.

(6) Bhao-Adhaya—the part which treats of action and movements in rhythm with singing and dancing.

(7) Arth-Adhaya—the part which treats of comprehension of tunes and times or rhythms.

Bhao-Adhaya is practically linked with *Nirt-Adhaya*, for it is the art of illustrating the songs and dances with the movements of arms and all parts of the body. *Arth-Adhaya* may be acquired by a theoretical study of the science and a constant hearing of it.

Indian music is formed of *Surs* (tones) and *Tālas* (times). Each is dependent upon the other for a complete arrangement of a tune sung or played.

The *Tālas* are executed on such instruments as the *Pakhavaj*, *Tabla*, etc.

The *Surs* (notes) from tunes which may either be played or sung on such instruments as *Vīna*, *Ta-oos*, etc.

*** The terms in this chapter have not been changed as they are the colloquial terms in use in northern India.**

The *Surs* (notes) are seven in number and are named individually : *Kharaj* or *Shadj*, *Rishabha*, *Gāndhāra*, *Madhyama*, *Panchama*, *Dhaivat*, *Nishadha* and collectively they are called *Sargam* ; and to simplify their use in music, they have abbreviated names to distinguish them, such as *Sa*, *Re*, *Ga*, *Ma*, *Pa*, *Dha*, *Ni*.

These *Surs* have interesting biographies, human and supernatural in composition.

They are human in having temperaments, costumes and colours, and like products of nature, they flourish in particular seasons. They are descended from Heavenly bodies and trace their lineage from above.

Certain *Surs* are dominant at certain stages of a man's life, they are produced from various parts of the body.

The *Surs* occur in certain animals from whom they are taken.

Those *Surs* which possess hot temperaments* have the mysterious faculty of curing those afflicted with rheumatism and such ailments, and vice-versa, provided they are sung by high-minded and noble souls, and at the specified† season of the year and hour of the day, when they should be sung ; then alone will the desired effect be obtained. Any violation of the prescribed law is regarded as sacrilege.

The seven notes are under the protection of the seven *Devatās* who preside over them.

INTERESTING CHRONICLES OF SURS (NOTES)

Kharaj or Sa. This *Sur* is under the protection of *Agni Deva*, and like *Panchama* does not lend itself to change into *Tīvra* (sharp) or *Kōmal* (flat), but is permanent.

It is connected with the first heaven and the planet called *Kamar* (moon in Arabic).

* Temperaments are astrological, as the various *Surs* are grouped under the rulership of the seven planets, and as the planets are, according to the canons of astrology, given rulership of the elements. The Sun and Mars are considered to be hot, as they rule the elements of fire, Jupiter and the Moon rule water, Venus and Mercury rule air, and Saturn rules the element of earth. Hence these various temperaments.

† Astrologically, the day is divided into twelve equal parts of daylight, and twelve equal parts of the night. This is done from exact sunrise to sunset, and from sunset to sunrise again. These part are given planetary rulerships, and each astrological hour may vary in length according to the latitude of the place and season, knowledge of which is very necessary to know the exact *Rāga* or *Rāginī* which is to be played or sung to produce the desired effect.

It has a happy temperament.

In effect it is cold and moist.

Its complexion is pink.

It is arrayed in most beautiful white garments and lovely ornaments.

Its seasons are—all the seasons of the year.

This note is produced from the abdomen.

Its sound has been taken from the cry of the bird *Ta-oos* (Peacock).

It is prevalent in the voice of the human being when he is seventy years old.

This tone is harmonious in all the *Rāgas* and *Rāginis*.

It has four *Surats* (semi-tones) or shades of tones, namely, *Tīvra*, *Kamod-vati*, *Manda* and *Chan-do-dhuti*. Rishabha or Re. This *Sur* is under the protection of the *Brahma Devata*.

This tone changes into *Tīvra* (sharp) or *Kāmal* (flat) as the occasion may require.

It is connected with the second heaven and the planet called *Retarid* (Mercury in Arabic). It has a happy temperament.

In effect it is cold and dry.

Its complexion is pale-green ; it is arrayed in a red costume and is decorated with beautiful ornaments.

Its season is the hot season.

This note is produced from the heart.

Its sound has been taken from the cry of the bird *Papīha*.

This note is prevalent in the voice of a human being when he is sixty years old.

It is harmonious in the tunes *Des*, *Kanhra*, etc., and quite unpleasant in *Malkaus*, *Hindole*, etc.

It has three *Surats* (shades of tones) *Dayati*, *Ranjani* and *Ragtika*. Gāndhar or Ga. This *Sur* is under the protecting Divinity *Sarasvati*.

This changes into sharp and flat as the occasion may require.

It is connected with the third Heavens and the planet called *Zuhrah* (Venus in Arabic).

It is of a sad temperament.

In effect it is cold and moist.

Its complexion is orange and is arrayed in crimson garments.

Its season is the hot weather.

This note is produced from the chest.

Its sound has been taken from the cry of the animal *Goos-fund.*

It is prevalent in the voice of a human being aged fifty.

It is pleasant in the tunes *Kalangra*, *Khamach*, etc., and is quite unpleasant in *Saranga.*

It has two *Surats*, *Se-ve* and *Kro-dhi.*

Madhyam or Ma. This *Sur* is under the protection of the God *Mahadev.*

It changes into sharp and flat.

It is connected with the fourth heaven and the planet called *Shams* (sun in Arabic).

It has a restless temperament.

In effect it is warm and dry.

Its complexion is pale pink. It is arrayed in reddish black garments and is prettily ornamented.

Its season is the rainy season.

It is produced from the throat.

Its sound has been taken from the cry of the bird *Saras* (Crane).

It is prevalent in the voice of a human being when he is forty years old.

This note is pleasant in *Malkaus*, *Bhairon*, etc., and is unpleasant in *Kalyan.*

It has four *Surats* : *Vajrika*, *Prasarini*, *Priti* and *Marjni.*

Pacnama or Pa. This note is under the protection of the Goddess *Lakshmi.*

It is connected with the fifth heaven and the planet called *Marrikh* (Mars in Arabic).

It has a passionate temperament.

In effect it is warm and dry.

Its complexion is red, and is arrayed in yellow garments.

Its season is the rainy weather.

This note is produced from the mouth.

Its sound has been taken from the cry of the bird *Koyal* (Cuckoo).

It is prevalent in the voice of a human being when he is thirty years old.

It sounds pleasant in the tunes *Todi-Asaori* and is quite unpleasant in *Malkaus*, *Hindole*, etc.

It has four *Surats* : *Ragta*, *Sandipani*, *Alapni*, *Rohiti*.

Dhaivat or Dha. This *Sur* is under the protection of *Ganesha*.

It changes into sharp and flat.

It is connected with the sixth heaven and the planet called *Mushtarī* (Jupiter in Arabic).

It has an equable temperament.

In effect it is warm and cold.

Its complexion is yellow, and it is arrayed in vermilion garments with lovely ornaments.

Its season is the cold weather.

It is produced from the palate

Its sound has been taken from the neighing of a horse.

This note is prevalent in the voice of a human being when he is twenty years old.

It is harmonious in *Bilāwal*, *Alaiya*, etc., and is inharmonious in *Zeelaf*, *Jogiya*, etc.

It has three *Surats* : *Mandati*, *Rohini*, *Ramya*.

Nishadha or Ni. This *Sur* is protected by *Surya*.

It is changeable into sharp and flat, according to the tune in which it occurs.

It is connected with the seventh heaven and the planet called *Zahol* (Saturn in Arabic).

It has a happy and passionate temperament.

In effect it is cold and dry.

Its complexion is dark ; it is arrayed in black garments and is most beautifully ornamented.

Its season is the cold weather.

It is produced from the nose.

Its sound has been taken from the trumpeting of an elephant.

This note is prevalent in the voice of a human being when he is ten years old.

It is pleasant in *Bihag*, *Puruj*, etc., and quite unpleasant in *So-rath*, etc.

It has two *Surats* : *Oogara* and *Sho-bhi-ni*.

DIVISIONS OF NOTES

To portray to our minds the most exquisite harmony which the shades of Tones form in Indian music by a cut and dried theory is out of the question. There are tones half-tones, quarter-tones and eighths of tones in it. The difference in these sounds as can be well imagined is so subtle and so exquisitely fine that before one has consciousness of one sound, it has merged into the other of its own accord, forming soft modulations and unexpected cadences. It is unutterably pure, classically beautiful and sublime in expression. These Shades of Tones correspond with the *Surats* previously mentioned.

There is a certain stage in each note, which is neither *Tīvra* (sharp) nor *Komal* (flat), but a sound in between the two. This sound or note is called the *Shudha Sur* and forms the central sound of a note. There are three notes in a higher key than the *Shudha;* and three notes in a lower key than the *Shudha;* and these together form the seven tones in one tone.

A tone which is one degree higher than the *Shudha* is called *Tīvra.*
A tone which is two degrees higher that the *Shudha* is called *Ta-Tīvra.*
A tone which is three degrees higher than the *Shudha* is called *Tām-Tīvra.*
A tone which is one degree lower than the *Shudha* is called *Kōmal.*
A tone which is two degrees lower than the *Shudha* is called *Ati-Kōmal.*
A tone which is three degrees lower than the *Shudha* is called *Shikari.*

These are the seven tones that divide the one tone. The subtlety and fineness of these sounds may better be imagined than written To an untrained ear these delicate shades of tone are meaningless and are hardly discernible. He is merely conscious of an exquisite flow of sounds, all blending into one another, making a graceful whole.

These seven notes correspond with the *Surats* already mentioned. These divisions of notes as well as the *Surats* as given in the ancient texts of Sanscrit works, are too complicated to be understood and one gets thoroughly puzzled. As a matter of fact, there are twenty-two *Surats* or shades of tone in one octave in Indian music ; and the difference in these is merely that of a hair-breadth, hardly distinguishable to the foreign ear in a melody. And yet it is these *Surats* which are of great importance in the formation of a tune and in retaining its individual and original character. They are distinct sounds and easily heard when a finished performer plays or sings them slowly in a scale, striking each note successively.

Asrekar of Poona has made out a very clever table, facilitating their comprehension and use in tunes, discarding some of the classical terms, and putting them in his own way which is simpler and easily understood.

ASREKAR'S TABLE OF TWENTY SURATS

Surats			*The tunes in which they occur.*
(1) Chan-do-vati or Sa.	This occurs in all the tunes.		
(2) Dayavati or Ati Komal Re.	do.	the tune	*Bhairon.*
(3) Ranjani or Komal Re.	do.	do.	*Bhaiveen.*
(4) Rag-Tika or Sudha Re.	do.	do.	*Bibhas.*
(5) (Seve) or Tivra Re. (Roudri)	do.	do.	*Yemen* and *Kalyan.*
(6) Kro-dhi or Ati Komal Ga.	do.	do.	*Todee.*
(7) Vaj-rika or Komal Ga.	do.	do.	*Bhairveen.*
(8) Prasarini or Madhya Ga.	do.	do.	*Malkaus.*
(9) Preti or Tivra Ga.	do.	do.	*Yemenkalyan.*
(10) Madrjani or Komal Ma.	do.	do.	*Bhairveen.*
(11) Kshiti or Madhya Ma.	do.	do.	*Poorbee.*
(12) Ragta or Tivra Ma.	do.	do.	*Yemenkalyan.*
(13) Sandipni or Tivratar Ma.	do.	do.	*Poorya.*
(14) Alapni or Sudha Pa.	do.	all the tunes where *Pa* is used.	
(15) Mandati or Ati Komal Dha.	do.	the tune	*Bhairon.*
(16) Rohini or Komal Dha.	do.	do.	*Bhairveen.*
(17) Rammya or Sudh Dha.	do.	do.	*Bibhas* *Malkaus.*
(18) Ugra or Tivra Dha.	do.	do.	*Yemenkalyan.*
(19) Shobhini or Ati Komal Ni.	do.	do.	*Gond Malad.*
(20) Tivra or Komal Ni.	do.	do.	*Bhairveen.*
(21) Kumudavati or Madhya Ni.	do.	do.	*Malkaus.*
(22) Mandha or Tivra Ni.	do.	do.	*Yemenkalyan.*

N.B.—The major scale in European music would correspond with the notes as follows : *Chandovati* or *Sa-Roudrī* or *Re-Prītī* or *Ga-Ragta* or *Ma-Alapni* or *Pa-Ugra* or *Dha Mandha* or *Ni.*

SAPTAKS (OCTAVES)

The seven notes in Indian music, *Sa*, *Re*, *Ga*, *Ma*, *Pa*, *Dha*, *Ni*, otherwise called the *Sargam* form a *Saptak* (octave). There are five *Saptaks*.

The lowest octave is called *Mandra Tar Saptak.*

The next lowest is called *Mandra.*

The notes of this *Saptak* are produced from the abdomen.

The medium octave is called *Madhyam Saptak.* The notes of this *Saptak* are produced from the throat.

The next highest octave is called *Tar-Saptak*, and the notes of this octave are produced from the head.

The highest octave is called *Tar-Tar Saptak.*

A qualified singer must produce the three *Saptaks* : *Mandra*, *Madhyam* and *Tar*, with ease.

The five *Saptaks* and even more may be played on the instrument *Been*

The ascending from the low notes to the high in a scale is termed *Rohi* and descending from the high notes to the low notes in the scale is called *Arohi* :

Sa, *Re*, *Ga*, *Ma*, *Pa*, *Dha*, *Ni*, *Sa* is *Rohi* and
Sa, *Ni*, *Dha*, *Pa*, *Ma*, *Ga*, *Re*, *Sa* is *Arohi.*

CHAPTER V

Tāla Adhaya

Tāla—Time or Rhythm is an important factor in the science of music, regulating the relative durations of musical sounds in singing, playing and dancing.

Mātra—is a unit of *Tāla* and varies in number in the different *Tālas*.

Zarb—is a stroke or beat denoting the division of *Mātras* in a *Tāla*.

Sum—The first or beginning point of a performance, and also the climax when the singer, player, or dancer with the drummer come to a happy termination and meet each other in perfect harmony and elicit applause.

Kāl—is an absence of the stroke at an appointed point.

Laya (Speed)—are regular intervals. These are of three kinds :

Bilampat—slow.
Madh—medium.
Dhurat—rapid.

The uniformity of time is broken by the performer changing the different *Layas* during the performance.

Also :

Tha—one half,
Baraber—equal,
Dooni—double,
Chongan—quadruple,
Ada—small and a half,
Savai—one and a quarter.

The *Tālas* or Rhythms are performed on the different varieties of drum, the most elaborate being the *Pakhavaj*. These drums are tuned to the keynote of the singer or player, and the *Thékas* or expressions are executed by the palms, fingers and even elbows of both the hands—also by sticks on the edge, middle and centres of the two circles that lie one within the other of the drums, and one gets such expressions or the actual initial letters such as capital *Ka*, *Ga*, *Gha*, *Ta*, *Tha*, *Da*, *Dha*, *Na*, *Ma*, *Ra*, *La*, etc. These are combined and out of these very initial or elementary letters and in the space of 16 *mātras* you get 65,535 combinations of *Thékas* called "*Purans*," by the same systematic and artistic arrangement, similar to that of the singer, player or dancer, when he takes up a theme and asserts his individuality by creating various embellishments to adorn music on the spur of the moment during the course of a performance.

The drummer plays the *Thèka* of a certain *Tāla* that is required and then goes on introducing the *parans* (combinations), keeping regard to the *Laya* and meets the singer, instrumentalist, or dancer on the *Sum* or climax of the beat, resulting in an unconscious pleasure and satisfaction to both the listener and player.

The ancient granthas indicate 35 *Jati Tālas* (Rhythms) based on restricted laws and 123 other varieties of *Tālas* in which the *mātras* vary from one to 74 in each *Tāla*, and the beat or *Zarb* varying from one to 18 in each *Tāla*.

The *Tālas* that are in vogue to-day in India are about two dozen, the *mātras* vary from 4 to 16 in each *Tāla*. These are as follows :

Kerava--Matras 4

MATRAS	1	2	3	4
THEKA	Dhagin,	Tinakdhin,	Tagin,	Tinakdhin.
ZARB	×			

Dadara—Matras 6

MATRAS	1	2	3	4	5	6
THEKA	Dhin	Dhin	Dha	Dha	Ti	Na
ZARB	×			o		

Pushtoo—Matras 7

MATRAS	1	2	3	4	5	6	7
THEKA	Ta	Ka	Dhin	Dha	Dha	Dha	Din
ZARB	×			2		3	

Rupaka—Matras 7

MATRAS	1	2	3	4	5	6	7
THEKA	Dhin	Dha	Trik	Dhin	Dhin	Dha	Trik
ZARB	×			2		3	

Sulfakta—Matras 10

MATRAS	1 2	3 4	5 6	7 8	9 10
THEKA	Dhin Dhin	Dha Tirkit	Dhin Dhin	Dha Tirkit	Tin Na
ZARB	×	0	2	3	0

Jhabtala—Matras 10

MATRAS	1 2	3 4 5	6 7	8 9 10
THEKA	Dhin Na	Dhin Dhin Na	Kit Ta	Dhin Dhin Na
ZARB	×	2	0	3

Khemta—Matras 12

MATRAS	1 2 3	4 5 6	7 8 9	10 11 12
THEKA	Dha Te Dhe	Na Te Ne	Ta Te Dhe	Na Te Ne
ZARB	×	2	0	3

Ektala—Matras 12

MATRAS	1 2	3 4	5 6	7 8	9 10	11 12
THEKA	Dhin Dhin	Dha Trik	Tu Na	Kat Ta	Dha Trik	Dhi Na
ZARB	×	0	2	0	3	4

Choutala—Matras 12

MATRAS	1 2	3 4	5 6	7 8	9 10	11 12
BOL	Dha Dha	Dhin Ta	Kata Ta	Dhin Ta	Tit Kit	Gid Gin
ZARB	×	0	2	0	3	4

Farodast—Matras 14

MATRAS	1 2	3 4	5 6	7 8	9 10	11 12 13 14
THEKA	Dhin Kirtik	Dhin Kirtik	Dhin Kirtik	Nighin Nighin	Dhin Kirtik	Dhin Na Kit Ta
ZARB	×	0	2	3	4	5

Adachoutala—Matras 14

MATRAS	1	2	3	4	5	6	7	8	9	10	11	12	13	14
THEKA	Dhin	Tirkid	Dhi	Na	Tu	Na	Kat	Ta	Tirkid	Dhi	Na	Dhi	Dhi	Na
ZARB	×		2		0		3		0		4		0	

Zumra—Matras 14

MATRAS	1	2	3	4	5	6	7	8	9	10	11	12	13	14
THEKA	Dhin	Dha	Tirkit	Dhin	Dhin	Dha	Tit	Tin	Na	Tirkit	Dhin	Dhin	Dha	Tit
ZARB	×			2				0			3			

Chachar—Matras 14

MATRAS	1	2	3	4	5	6	7	8	9	10	11	12	13	14
THEKA	Dha	Dhin	In	Dha	Ge	Tin	In	Na	Tin	In	Dha	Ge	Dhin	In
ZARB	×			2				0			3			

Dipchandi—Matras 14

MATRAS	1 2 3	4 5 6 7	8 9 10	11 12 13 14
THEKA	Dhin Dhin S	Dha Ga Tin S	Ta Tin S	Dha Ga Dhin S
ZARB	×	2	0	3

Dhamar—Matras 14

MATRAS	1 2 3 4 5	6 7	8 9 10	11 12 13 14
THEKA	Ga Dhe Ta Dhi Ta	Dha S	Ghe Te Ta	Ti Ta Ta S
ZARB	× (Sum)	2	0 (Kaal)	3

Tilawada—Matras 16

MATRAS	1 2 3 4	5 6 7 8	9 10 11 12	13 14 15 16
THEKA	Dha Trik Dhin Dhin	Dha Dha Tin Tin	Ta Trik Dhin Dhin	Dha Dha Dhin Dhin
ZARB	×	2	0	3

Trital—Matras 16

MATRAS	1	2	3	4	5	6	7	8	9	10	11	12	13	14	15	16
THEKA	Ta	Dhin	Dhin	Dha	Ta	Dhin	Dhin	Dha	Dha	Tin	Tin	Ta	Ta	Dhin	Dhin	Dha
ZARB	×				2				0				3			

CHAPTER VI

Ast Adhya

(rules for musical instruments)

Singing is considered to be the highest form of musical culture in India. The person who has a beautiful voice and a clear understanding is specially favoured. Singing is not perfect unless accompanied by instruments for *Tāla* (time) and *Sur* (intonation).

The next in order of accomplishment in music is *Vādan* (playing).

Musical instruments in India are of infinite variety and structure, beautiful and artistic. They are classed under separate types and go under four great headings. Their functions are varied. Some are meant only for accompanying purposes to songs, and have no special bearing, significance, or beauty when played by themselves—such as *Sarangi*, *Tublā*, *Pakhawāj*, *Tamburā*, etc. Others are important instruments and are played by themselves, and are full of richness, beauty and intricacy, such as the *Vīna*, *Sitar*, *Sarode*, *Bānsari* etc.

The following are the four headings under which all the musical instruments of India come : *Tut*, *Betat*, *Ghun* and *Sekhar*.

Tut comprises those instruments that are strung with brass or steel wires or with silken or cotton cords, and are struck, either by a piece of wood, ivory, the finger nails or a small contrivance made of wire, in the shape of a finger-end called *Mijrāb*. These instruments are the *Vīna*, *Sarode*, *Tamburā*, etc.

Betat are those instruments that have skins stretched in the hollow circular form at one end, and are played with a bow, such as the *Sarangi*, *Taus*, *Dilruba*, etc.

Ghun are the species of drum-like instruments, struck by the hand or a stick of wood, like *Pakhawāj*, *Tublā*, *Dhol*, *Nakkārī*, etc.

Sekhar. These are the pipe-like instruments blown by the mouth either by full or half breaths, like *Nafeeri Bansri*, *Poongi*, *Senai*, etc.

There are five instruments which, if mastered in learning to play them, facilitate the easy management of all other instruments, and these are the *Vina*, *Mrudung*, *Senai Sarangi* and *Rubab*.

(1) By acquiring the art of playing the *Vīna* to perfection, *Sitar* and *Tamburā* and all such stringed instruments, are most easily manipulated. The *Vīna* being the most intricate of Indian musical instruments.

(2) By becoming an expert on the *Pakhawāj*, the *Tublā*, *Dhol Duff*, *Chhamp*, *Dhoomus*, etc., may be played without much effort. These are all the species of the drum, and *Pakhawāj* is the most difficult of its kind, musicians have individual methods of playing it ; some strike them by the hand and some by rods and so on, but the beat and time is more or less similar. *Pakhawāj* has the most numerous and intricate beats of all.

(3) Of all the pipe-like instruments, *Senai* is the most difficult, and if this is learnt to perfection all the other instruments of its kind, like *Tota-gazi*, *Bānsri Pungi*, *Nai*, *Bhīr*, etc., are easily acquired. All are blown by the mouth, either by half or full breaths and the fingers are pressed on and lifted off the openings, to produce notes.

(4) Sarangi is a stringed instrument, played by a bow and is the most difficult of its kind ; so that if it is played well the other instruments of its class, like *Taus*, *Do-Tara*, etc., are very easily acquired.

(5) The fifth instrument which if learnt to perfection facilitates the learning of other instruments of its kind is *Rubab*. If this is learned with excellence, *Sarode Sur-Vīna*, *Jantri* and such are easily learnt.

The authorship of the most ancient system of music of India is attributed to the *Mahadeva*, who invented the *Vīna* and *Damru* for his own pastime. *Vīna* is the musical representation of the Goddess Pārvati and very pretty legends record the origin of this instrument.

Those that are invented by the deities are regarded as sacred and the profoundest respect is paid to them.

Ganeshji, the pot-bellied god, invented the classical drum *Mrudang* or *Pakhawāj*, after the style of *Damru*, and from *Pakhawāj* were invented *Tublā*, *Dholak*, *Dhoomus*, *Chhamp* and other drum species. Many instruments of a

PAKHAWAJ

SINGHAR

Facing page 52.

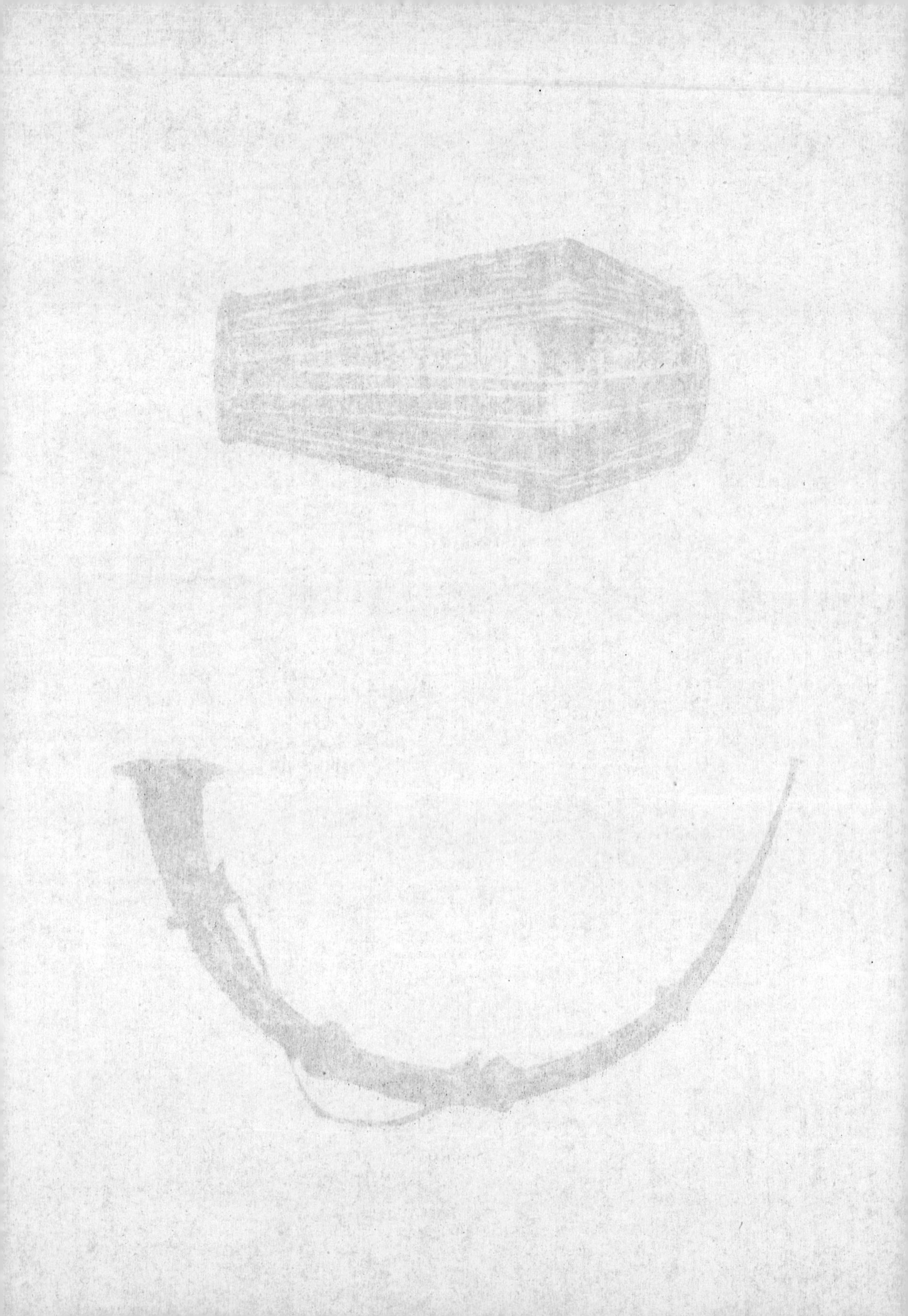

simpler construction and beauty followed the *Vīna* and like the *Sur-Vīna*, *Sur Singar*, *Tamburā*, *Sitar*, etc.

The fabled *Bānsri*, was the invention of the Love-god Krishna, who intoxicated the milkmaids (*gopis*) with its sweet and enticing strains.

Senai was invented by *Hakīm Bu Ali Senai*, and named after him ; *Uns*, *Tota-Gazi*, *Aadh-guz*, etc., followed in the later years.

Sarangi is also the invention of a *Hakīm* of a comparatively much later period. *Do-Tara*, *Kamancha*, *Taus* and similar instruments, came into existence after.

The stirring and appealing *Nai* was the creation of *Omar Aiyyar*, noted for his clever pranks.

Algoza, Pungi and such came into practice later.

The majestic drum *Nakkārā* was played before royalty or in times of war. Smaller instruments of its kind were made later.

(*a*) The following are the instruments that are played by the fingers and are fitted with metal wires :

Rudra Vīna is a glorious heirloom of ages, and the king of instruments invented by the originator of Indian music, *Mahadeva*. The beautiful legend attached to its origin runs thus :

Mahadeva once saw *Pārvati* reposing most gracefully, her fragrant breath breathing soft music, her exquisite bosom rising and falling in rhythm, her arms and wrists laden with bangles, causing music by their motion.

Mahadeva, intoxicated by the ravishing vision, gazed at it long and silently, and retained it in his memory. The lovely picture disturbed his mental equilibrium, and left him no peace, until at last it settled into a definite and exquisite vision in his mind by its deep impression, resulting in the invention of the musical instrument, the unrivalled *Vīna*.

The long neck represents the straight lithe figure of *Pārvati*. The two gourds her well-shaped, ivory-like breasts, and the metal frets, her bracelets, and most exquisite of all, the sound, par excellence, her rhythmic breathing.

To handle a *Vīna* is a most arduous task, a life-time of practice can alone produce a master-player of the instrument. It is played seated with folded legs, with one gourd resting on the left shoulder, and the other resting on the folded legs. The style of performing on the *Vīna* is mostly in the *Alap-Chari* ;

and *Pakhawāj* accompaniment is the correct thing for it. The wires are struck with *Mizrābs* and nails, kept long for the purpose, of the right hand. The left-hand fingers are pressed on the fixed frets, to produce the different notes.

It is a very complicated and intricately-made instrument, handsomely ornamented, with inlaid ivory and artistic designs in gold and silver painted on its exterior, and is a very expensive instrument.

Sarasvati Vīna, so called after the goddess of Music and Learning, Sarasvati, who is invariably represented in paintings as holding the instrument in her hands. It is somewhat similar to the *Vīna* in form, having a finger-board fitted with metal frets, and a sloping gourd at the bottom, and a gourd on top, and the head of a carved lion at one end.

It is the instrument of Southern India, and is accompanied by *Pakhawāj*. It is played seated and held slanting, pressed with the right arm. The wires are struck with the fingers of the right hand, and the left-hand fingers run up and down pressing the bars unsupported. This is a comparatively easier *Vīna* of the two.

It is beautifully carved and worked with gold and silver.

Sitar (lit. *Seh-tar* which means three wires) is a very clever invention of *Amir Khusru*, whose name is so well-known in the musical world of India. It has always been one of the most popular instruments. A particular style of music is played upon it, and one which is called *Jore* and *Gut Toda*. The drum *Tublā* accompanies the *Sitar*.

It is invariably highly ornamented and is played seated—the right arm pressing the gourd ; the neck is held slanting. On the first finger of the right hand a *mizrāb* is worn which strikes the wires, the left fingers press the movable frets to form the notes.

Ektāra is a modest little instrument of one wire, only used by wandering mendicants, who sing *Bhajans* (hymns) on it. A bit of skin is stretched in the hollow circular form and on the neck or rod one wire is strung. That one wire is struck at intervals to accompany the song. The sound is exceedingly pathetic.

Tamburā was invented by the *Rishi Nārada*. It has a sloping gourd and a long neck strung by four wires only. The object of this instrument

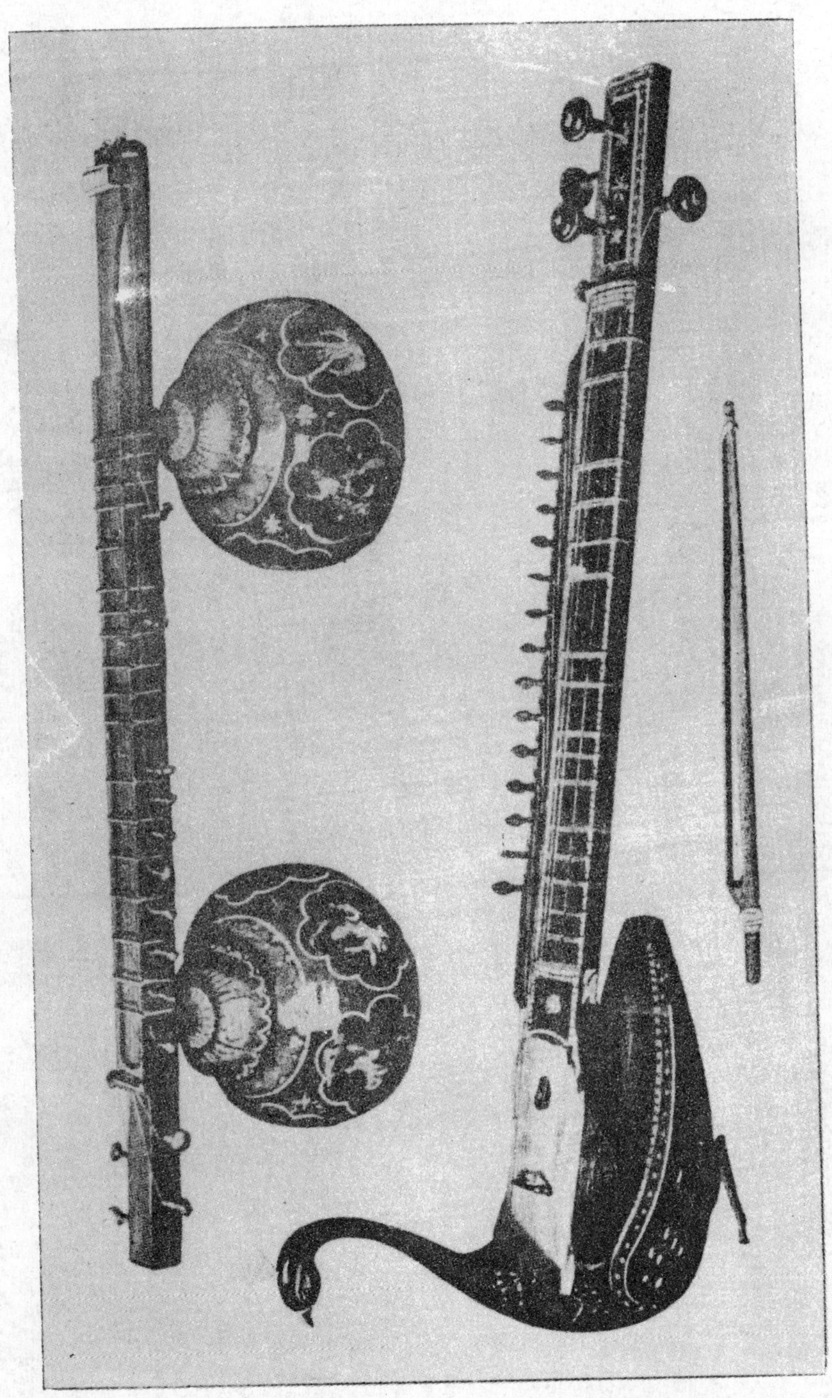

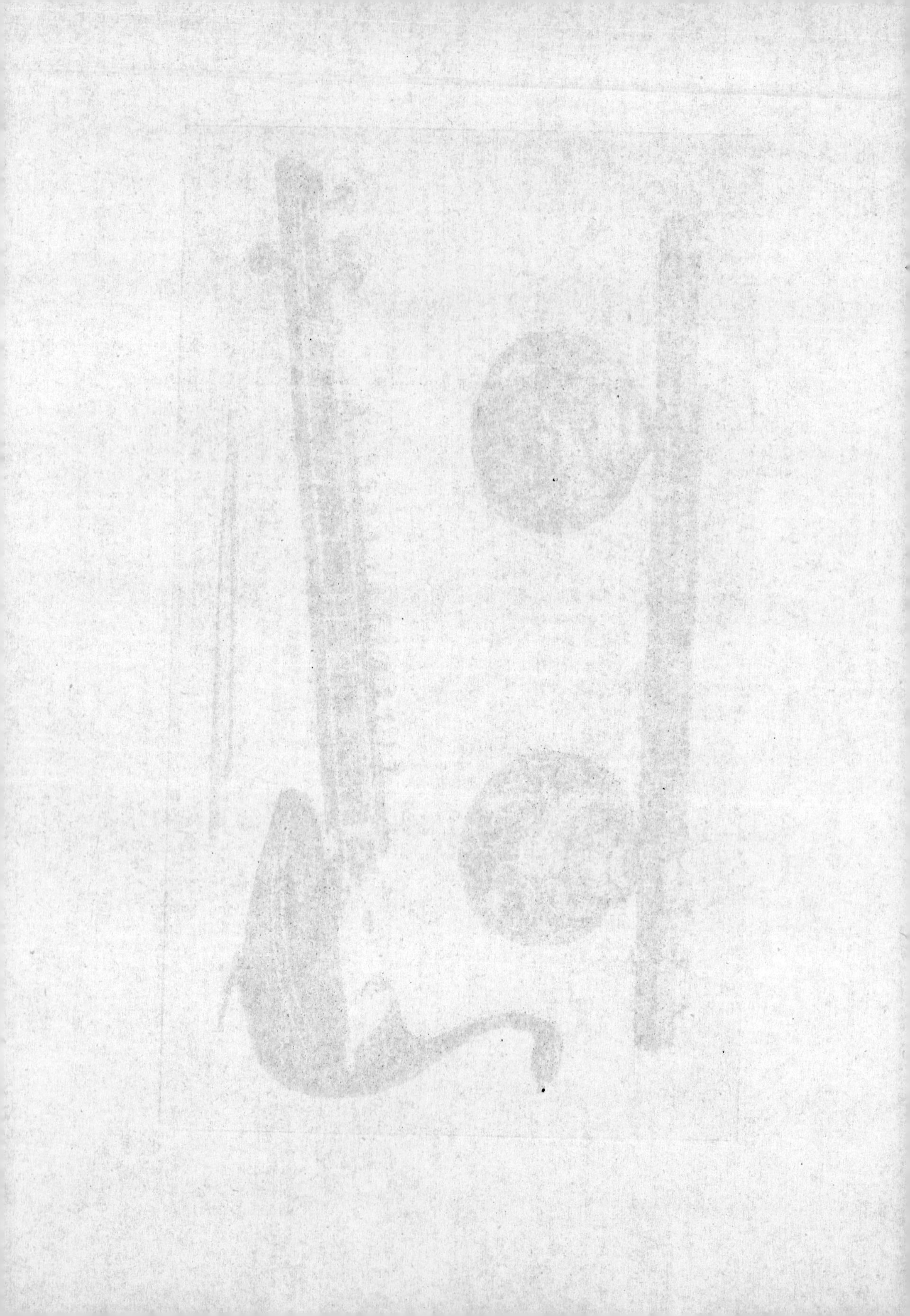

merely to accompany songs and other instruments that are played individually.

It is played seated ; the gourd rests between the legs and the neck rests on the right shoulder. The first finger of the right hand strikes the four chords at regular intervals in rhythm with the tune.

A singer is like a fish out of water without his ***tamburā.***

(*b*) The following instruments are played with a bow and have metal bars for the guidance of notes.

Kamancha. This is made entirely of wood and a skin stretched on a lower portion ; the upper portion is just like a *Sitar*, and the lower like a *Sarangi* ; and like the *Sarangi* it is played with a bow.

It is mostly used in the Punjab as accompaniment to songs.

Taus, so called because of its beautiful colour and shape like that of a peacock. It is painted in all the metallic shades of the beautiful bird. Its tail is the straight finger-board, fitted with movable frets just like the *Sitar*, and the lower portion is like the head of the fascinating bird. It is played seated with a bow.

Dilruba. This is similar to *Taus*. The only difference is that the *Taus* has got the head of a peacock, and this has not. It is played seated with a bow.

(*c*) The following instruments are played with a bow and have no metal bars.

Sarangi, the violin of the East. Its tone is delicate and sweet, and is quite a necessary asset to singing and dancing. It is a very popular instrument all over India. All the fluctuations, inflections and variations of the human voice are most exquisitely produced on this instrument. A skin is stretched on the lower squarish portion and two groupings of wires are placed upon the surface one on the other. The upper ones are played with a bow. It has no bars, so that the notes are produced on the surface wires. It is played standing or seated just as the occasion may require.

It is the invention of a ***Hakīm*** of former times. The story goes on to say that a ***Hakīm*** was once travelling on foot and worn out with heat and fatigue, rested beneath a huge tree. Suddenly some sweet strains of music reached his ears ; he listened astonished, attentively, and searched in vain from whence the sound came, until at last looking up he discovered the object of his search.

The dried skin of a dead monkey was stretched between two branches entangled with its dried guts, and the wind blowing through it caused melodious sounds. He carefully removed the skin and guts, replaced them on a construction of wood and after some years of labour, with due modifications and additions, completed the present-day *Sarangi*.

Jaunpuri Sarangis are the most famous.

Sazinda. This is a quaint-looking instrument, invented by *Guru Amardās*, the founder of the city of Amritsar, whose temple in that city is so well-known. It is made entirely of wood, and has an oval, hollow form beneath and a strip of wood across on which wires are strung.

It is placed in the same position as the *Sarangi* and is played with a bow. The fingers are pressed on the wires to form notes.

Hindustani Dotāra. This two-stringed instrument is like a simplified miniature *Sarangi*, used by the peasantry It is called *Do-Tāra*, which literally means two wires.

Marwari Dotāra. This is only used in *Marwar*. It has a gourd of a half coco-nut, with a skin stretched over it. The neck is made of wood, on which are strung two wires. It is played with a bow.

(*d*) The following instruments have four wires, have no bars and are played with a pectrum. They are all very difficult to learn and are played seated.

Rubab. This is supposed to be the invention of *Sikandar Zulqarnein*.* It is made of wood, and skin stretched on the lower portion. It has two groups of wires one below the other. The surface has got four wires, and seven below, called *Taraps*. It is played with a triangular piece of wood and the notes are created on the wires.

Sarode. Is similar in construction to *Rubab*, but different in form. It has a circular hollow gourd, with skin stretched over it and the neck ends in a hook-like arrangement on the top.

Chārtār literally means four wires. This instrument is very akin to *Sarode* in construction but differs slightly in shape.

* Alexander the Great.

Sur-Vīna was invented by *Kalé Sāhib*, a prince of Delhi. It is like the *Sitar* in shape without the bars. The surface is covered with a thin plate of steel. It has two groups of wires, four on the surface and seven below.

Sur Singār. Like *Rubab*, it is made of wood and skin stretched on the lower portion that widens into an ovalish elongation. Owing to its extreme complications, there are very few musicians who attempt to play on this instrument. *Bahadur Sen*, one of the Court musicians of *Rampur*, is an expert on the *Rubab* and *Sur Singār*.

Tarab. This is a quaint instrument, made out of one piece of wood ; and skin stretched on the widened lower portion. It has many wires but no bars. The method of playing it is peculiar. It is laid flat on the ground and struck by a long thin piece of semicircular strip of wood.

(*e*) The following are pipe-like instruments blown by the mouth.

Algūza. It is a flute made of bamboo and black wood. It is slightly wider at the bottom than the top, and has seven apertures at equal intervals.

Pair of Algūza. These are two pipes of similar kind blown at one time and are used by the peasantry.

Nai has been the theme of all the poets and love-ditties ; it is the invention of *Omar Aiyyar*, to ensnare maidens with its magic sounds. It is an exact facsimile of the barrel of a gun, with seven openings.

Bānsri. Is the creation of the Love god, *Krishna Kanhaiya*, to entangle the *gopis* (milk-maids) in its charmed meshes. He succeeded in his object, for we have endless legends and songs, depicting the surrender of lovely maids, in spite of themselves.

Its sacred notes may be heard through the practice of *Yoga* (meditation). It is accompanied by the Duff.

Sankh is very rare and sacred. No place of worship is without this *Conch*.

It is the manifestation of sound in nature. *Sankh* is a species of shell, upside down in shape. In all the temples and shrines, the *Conch* is first blown and then the place entered. It has one shrill note only, and if placed in a windy position the sound is created automatically.

Sankhnāda, or the sound of the *Conch*, is said to be heard in *Yoga*.

Singhra. This is really a horn of a deer, which is blown in the temples, and is thus considered sacred.

Turai is made entirely of brass and is played with *Duff*.

Bheer is one of the most ancient flutes of mythological interest. It was played in the marriage of *Mahadeva* and *Pārvati*. It is made entirely of copper, and has a shrill sound.

Karna is a heavy curved pipe awkward to hold. It is blown hard and is played in a band, on important occasions—like war, marriage and such other big festivals. It is entirely made of brass and its sound is harsh and loud.

Pungi. This is a flute-like instrument used by the snake charmers for fascinating and training snakes. The sound is supposed to exercise great power over them.

It is composed of a dried gourd with an opening at the narrow end. Two thin and smooth, round, *Singāpuri* bamboos, with seven holes, are attached in the centre of the gourd below. Two human hairs are inserted in the pipes, and attached with wax. The big opening in the narrow portion of the gourd is blown by the mouth, and notes and tunes produced.

It is extraordinary how the weird sound of a *Pungi* affects serpents.

The snake charmer sits on the floor, playing a monotonous tune, swaying his body to and fro in a circular movement. The serpent gets strangely fascinated by the movement. It raises its head, and unconscious of all his surroundings, follows the snake charmer, bewitched. It sways its body and moves circularly. The notes getting louder, the charm of music so fascinating the snake, until it gets such a hold of it that it seems to become the very embodiment of the tune, breathing the melody with its rhythmic motions. The snake charmer stops the music. The spell broken, the snake drops down fatigued and gradually glides back into his place.

Murchang. This is a strange instrument. It is entirely made of thin strips of wire, in a fork-like arrangement. The central strip is elongated and curled at the end. It is held in the left hand. The central portion is held quite close to the mouth and certain expressions like *Dar Dir*, etc., are whispered musically over the fork. The right hand taps the curled end in rhythm. The sound is soft and delicious. In some parts of India it is quite a popular pastime.

Uns. This flute-like instrument is played by a band of four people, called the *Roushan Chauki Walé*, comprising two *Uns* players, one drummer, who beats on the *Champ*, and one bell-ringer who shakes the *Jhun Jhuna* in rhythm.

This band is played on festive occasions, and precedes the bridegroom in a marriage procession or goes in advance of a nobleman's cortège.

The construction of *Uns* is as follows. A tube ot seven holes is inserted into a cast cup of metal, and three strange little contrivances are held together with silk strings. They are fitted into one another on the mouth of the tube. The first is a metal needle, which is adjusted half-way in the tube. A disc of ivory, with a hole in the centre is fitted into this needle, and lastly a blade of a rare species of grass called *Pālā*, is settled carefully on top. The grass is soaked for an hour and then the *Uns* is ready for use.

Senai. The remarkable invention of *Hakeem Bu Ali Senai*. It is customary in India for the pupils to make a little offering and prayers, in the name of the inventor, before making a start to learn.

Senai is more or less similar to *Uns* in appearance. Its tube is narrower on the top, and widens at the bottom. Affixed in a cup, both tube and cup are made of blackwood. The metal needle, ivory disc, and blade of grass are adjusted on top as in *Uns*, only they vary in size.

This wonderful grass called *Pālā* is cultivated in a special region, with the greatest care. It is white or red, very flexible, and only used for the purpose of *Senai* and such instruments. All the tunes, with their fluctuations and variations, are very finely executed on this.

Senai is played in the temples and in a band called *Noubat*.

Noubat literally means nine performers. Two *Senaichis* (*Senai* players), two *Nakkarchis* (drummers), one *Jhanj* Ringer (bell ringer), one *Karnaichi* (*Karnai* player), one *Damama* (drum beater), one *Baridar* (attendant to warm the drums and fill the hookas for the party), and one *Jamadar* (conductor and leader of the band).

Noubat was a band exclusively organized for the dignity and majesty of the kings and noblemen, dead or living, and placed on the gateway of the palaces, mansions, mausoleums, tombs, etc., of royalty, in recognition of their presence therein, living or dead.

The custom is widely prevalent in India.

Noubat is played eight times during the twenty-four hours, at an interval of every three hours.

In olden times it was used for martial music in battle, and most stirring anecdotes are related of famous leaders of *Noubat*, who stimulated the warriors on the battlefields with bravery and courage.

Sangur and *Bhallun* are most brilliant names in the history of India's fighting days. Their spirited performance inspired the warriors with fresh energy and confidence to face the enemy over and over again. *Bhallun* and *Sangur* fell fighting on the battlefield, and were buried on the spot they fell.

A pilgrimage is made to the tombs by all the musicians of this class ; prayers and offerings are made to their respective names.

The legend says that the sticks with which they beat the drums were entombed. And the myth is that after some time they grew into beautiful trees shading their graves and yielding most delicious fruit.

(*f*) The following are the drum species, struck either by the hand or stick. These are only used for keeping the *Tāla* (time). The *Tāla* is a very complicated factor in Indian music and varies considerably with each tune.

The drum *Pakhawaj* has got nearly two or three hundred varieties of beats for each *Tāla*, and it is quite an ordinary thing for a finished *Pakhawaj* player to go on playing varied beats for a number of days.

Pakhawaj was invented by god *Ganésh*, and is the classical drum or India. It is the most difficult of its kind. It is only accompanied on *Dhurpad* and *Hori* style of songs, also with classical dancing, and the *Vīna*. It is in the shape of a barrel, and made of one piece of *Bir* wood, with skins stretched on either side. On one side black ink is applied and on the other the dough. It helps the dash of tone, and makes it rich in sound. The skins are strung with cords which are loosened and tightened according to the voice of the singer. The variety of sounds that are produced on the *Pakhawaj* is nothing short of a marvel.

Sometimes it is the booming of guns, sometimes it is thunder, sometimes it is nasal, sometimes it is the cry of birds, animals, and so on.

The beats of the *Pakhawaj* are first produced vocally and the same wording is reproduced on the drum ; each beat has got a name of its own, and the knowledge of them requires life-long study.

They are composed of such expressions as *Kit Tika*, *Giddi*, *Ghun*, *Tuk Dhikat*, *Dha*, etc.

It is wonderful how the very words are executed, as if somebody was repeating them.

Tubla Bāyén is the invention of *Sudhar Khan Dhari*, and is a very popular drum, of a lighter and easier nature to play than the *Pakhawaj*.

In appearance it is like *Pakhawaj*, equally divided into two parts. The construction is also more or less similar. It is either played squatted on the floor or standing, with both hands on the two parts, *Tubla* and *Bāyén*.

The beats are as follows : *Dha*, *Dhin*, *Dinna*, *Turkat*, *Kittack*, etc.

Manjera. These are metal cups of extremely pleasant sounds attached to each other with a loose piece of string and mostly played in a rhythm with a *Tubla*. Both the cups are held in the fingers, one heavier than the other and struck at intervals. Even this tiny little instrument has various beats and is struck with a particular method.

Dhoomus and Champ. These are two funny little drums, one for the right hand and one for the left. They are earthenware cups covered with skins, and encased in a cage of cords, and hung low from the neck of the player on either sides with strings. It accompanied the flute *Uns*, in the band of *Roushan Chouki Walé*.

Nakkara. The royal drum. It accompanies the *Senai* in the band *Noubat*. They are two in number, one smaller than the other. The smaller is called *Zeel* and is placed on the right-hand side ; and the larger one is called *Nar*, and is placed on the left side. The drummer takes two sticks in both hands and goes on striking according to the time and tune required, sometimes striking both with equal beats on each, and sometimes unequally, and at other times each stick strikes a drum with equal or unequal beats.

They are extremely large, made of metal, in the shape of kettle-drums used in the cavalry at the present day, with thick hides stretched on their surface. The sound is deep and loud, majestic and imposing.

Dhol is a barrel-shaped drum, played by women called *Domnis* on festive occasions, accompanied by songs suited to the occasion. It is easy and vulgar.

Tubla is a flat drum made of metal or clay with a skin stretched on it and struck with two sticks.

Marfa is more or less similar to the above and is struck with one stick. *Marfa* and *Tasha* are both played in a band at weddings, etc.

Jhanj is a castanet species made of metal.

Duff is another drum made of wood, with skin stretched over it. It accompanies two *Bānsris* and one *Tarai* in a band.

Dairu is the oldest drum of India, invented by *Mahadeva*. It is made of wood and skins stretched on either side and is struck by two sticks, one in each hand.

It is played in *Rajputana*.

Daira is a round flat drum, struck by the hand and played in bands.

Khanjari is a round flat drum played by both hands.

Daphra is a magnified *Khanjari*, played in the Holi festival in *Marwar*.

Dholak, simplified beats of *Pakhawaj* and *Tubla*, are played on this drum.

Kartāl is a pair of wooden castanets with little bells attached to them. It accompanies *Bhajans* (hymns) or mournful songs on sad occasions.

Jaltarang. These are sixteen china cups, arranged in a row and fitted with sufficient quantity of water to form the scale of notes, and are struck by two curved rods. The sound is more or less choppy, and the style of the *Gut Toda* of the *Sitar* is executed on this to perfection. It is accompanied by the *Sitar*.

This is a rough sketch of the well-known instruments. There are very many more of lesser importance belonging to different provinces, districts and villages. They have their own distinct music and songs.

The music of South India is quite distinct and has its own instruments, *Rāgas* and *Tālas*.

RĀGA BHAIRAON

Facing page 63.

CHAPTER VII

Rāga Adhya

Classification of Tunes. The order in which the tunes of the *Hanuman Māth* are classified is as follows :

They are divided into six *Rāgas* (male tunes). Each *Rāga* has its own five *Rāginīs* (female tunes) and eight *Putrās* (sons), and their eight *Bharyas* (wives), making in all one hundred and thirty-two tunes.

The important tunes are the six *Rāgas* and thirty *Rāginīs* ; the rest, ninety-six in number, are minor tunes, though some of these are as beautiful and melodious.

The *Rāgas* display the most exquisite form of musical conception. They are rich, heavy, melodious and of a highly classical order, and a devotional vein of spirituality is found in all of them.

They touch the deepest emotional chords of the human soul, and transport one to a higher and nobler realm.

The *Rāgas* have still retained their notes of original purity, notwithstanding the ravages of time and crudities of man ; nothing seems to have disturbed or affected their sublimity of expression and divine conception.

They are very difficult of execution, and none but the most accomplished musicians or profound masters comprehend the varied and numerous technicalities which go to make them complete, and who alone dare venture to perform them.

The *Rāginīs* are perhaps of a comparatively softer nature, though some are equally rich and deep in feeling and quite as difficult to perform. These classical tunes vary in the numbers of notes they possess in the octaves to form their scales.

In some tunes all the seven notes occur. These are termed *Sampuran*. In others only six notes of the octave form to make a scale and these are called *Khadao*, and some have only five or less notes of the octave which complete their scale, these are termed *Odhao*.

VARIOUS METHODS OF SINGING TUNES

There are various methods in which a tune may be sung or played in Indian music.

Dhrupad. A *Dhrupad* of any classical tune may be sung provided the performer is able to do it. It is very ancient. It is a manly and heavy way of singing, and is the most difficult of all the methods. *Dhrupad* is that style of singing which comprises dwelling upon each note with masterful control for some moments.

The "Division of Notes" in the previous chapter has shown how extremely fine and subtle is the space of sound allowed differentiating one note from the other. The slightest vibration in the voice tends to produce a *Surti* (shade of tone). Each note therefore, should be struck in its purity and richness of sound and dwelt upon clearly and distinctly. So that the power of retention with correct intonation, and with absolute control, is the first step of most vital importance. to be learnt in singing a *Dhrupad*, and is extremely difficult.

When the notes of a *Dhrupad* of any *Rāga* are struck with that accuracy and precision which it demands, a strange tremor overpowers one, so that one is conscious of nothing but the sound divine, that fills the atmosphere and holds one in a magic spell. Each note is sung clearly and distinctly in its purity, with magical effect, and retained in its own glory as long as the power of the performer will allow.

Its theme is generally historical or religious. It is never sung quickly, but invariably in *Bilampat* or *Muddha lai*, i.e., first or second speed.*

Dhrupad singing is divided into four equal parts.

The first part is called *Asthai*. The opening notes of a tune are shown in this part

* There are three speeds in which a song may be sung or played:

1st Speed.	*Bilampat* (slow).	*Vilamba Kala.*
2nd Speed	*Maddh* (medium).	*Madhya Kala.*
3rd Speed.	*Dhurat* (rapid).	*Durta Kala.*

Rāga Mégh

Facing page 64.

The second part is called *Antra.* All the notes that occur in the tune are sung in this portion.

The treatment of the higher notes of the tune is shown in the third part called *A-bhog.*

The last part is called *Sanchari.* It was against the royal etiquette of the former days to sing any other style of tunes, excepting *Dhrupad* in *darbars. Dhrupad* singing is also called the *Khandari Bani.* It is the most difficult mode of execution and one which is restricted to only a very few musical families in India.

Rāja Mān Tanwar, 1486-1516, was the inventor of *Dhrupad.*

Naik Beyjoo, the famous singer, lived in his time. After the death of the *Raja, Beyjoo* went to the court of *Sultan Bahadur of Guljarat,* and in his reign invented a new *Todi,* which is known as *Bahaduri Todi.* It is a beautiful melody.

Sadra is something like the *Dhrupad,* but sung with the quick rhythm of *Jhaptad.* The subjects of the songs are military and sometimes eulogistic.

Hori These beautiful songs contained the love stories of *Krishna,* the god of love, and the *gopis.* The method of singing them is most fascinating, but most difficult. They are performed on the intricate unequal *Tāla* (rhythm) of Dhamar.

Dhrupad, *Saadra* and *Hori* singing are the most difficult styles, and eminent musicians disdain to perform by other methods.

Khyal. A *Khyal* of any classical tune may be sung. Unlike *Dhrupad,* each note merges into the other in quick succession. Wave after wave of delicious ethereal melodies float in the air. Floods of scales succeed one another, forming most exquisite combinations. And the effect is divine, owing to the rapid rise and fall of the scales. Trills, variations, tremors and all such productions of the voices have full play in this kind of singing. *Khyal* singing was invented by *Sultan Hussain Sherki,* in the fifteenth century, and brought to a state of perfection by *Sadaranga,* the *Durbar Singer* of *Mohammad Shah* of *Delhi.*

Sultan Hussain Sherki was the inventor of many beautiful melodies, such as *Jaunpoori, Hussain Kanhra, Hussain Todi,* which are still popular.

Tappa. These were originally sung by the camel and mule drivers in the

Punjab, in which they related the story of *Heera* and *Ranji*. *Shori*, the famous singer in the Court of *Asaf-ud-dowlah*, the King of Oudh, put new life and soul into it, and converted the simple ditty of the desert into a cultivated form of singing.

Baz Khani method of music was invented by *Baz Bahadur*, the king of *Malwa*. There are many lovely songs relating his passion for the beautiful *Rupmati*.

Baz Bahadur and *Rupmati* have also been a favourite subiect with the artists.

The fantastic *Amir Khusru*, poet, musician, minister, statesman, soldier, in the reign of the *Tughlaks*, 1295-1316, was so enamoured of Indian music and became such a great master in the art that even *Naik Gopal*, the great musician of the period, acknowledged him as a great master of his art. He introduced a sweet blend of the Persian mode of tune and modes and invented new melodies like *Gara*, *Sar Parda*, *Zeeluf*, etc.

In this reign *Paraband* and *Chand* were sung in *Brig Bhāsha*, the poet *Kushru*, who was unable to appreciate the classical Sanskrit, resorted to the soft melody of Persia in compromise.

Tarana, Koul, Naksh, Gul, etc.

Koul was sung with *Kawali Tāla* in Persian, similar to *Kalbana*, *Naksh* and *Gul*, the theme was generally *Sufism*.

Tarana was invented by *Amir Khusru*, certain expressions like *Yala*, *Lom*, *Tom*, *Non*, *Dani* and also Persian couplets are inserted in *Tarana*. Unlike *Alāp* this is sung to *Tāla*.

Alāp. This is to sing the melody of songs by inserting such expressions as *Aaar*, *Te*, *Ray*, *Re*, *Nom*, *Ta*, etc., instead of the real words of the song, without *Tāla*.

Sargam. This is to sing the tune of the song by the notes of the song, instead of the words. Such as *sa*, *re*, *ga*, *ma*, etc.

Tarwat. This is to sing the tune of the song by inserting the expressions of the *Tubla* (the drum-like instrument to keep time), and not the words of the song, such as *Dhirkat*, *Dirkat*. *Dar*, *Dhina*.

Chatrang, lit. means four parts. A mixture of *Alāp Sargaā Taranā* an *Tarwat* expressions are used in this.

Rāga Hindole

Facing page 66.

It is difficult to perform ; therefore it is not a popular mode of singing.

Bhajan. These are pathetic religious songs of appealing nature, sung by *Yogis* (ascetics) on the strange weird instrument called the *Ektara*, also by a band of devotees in a temple.

The recital is led by a leader followed by the followers in a chorus—*Pad*, *Kirtans*, also of sacred character.

These musical performances relate the stories. Heroes, gods and goddesses performed individually or by a circle of ascetics on special or religious occasions in temples or homes.

Thumri. These are extremely pretty little songs and are very popular and delightful, sung by all in India. They are generally composed in *Brij-Bhasha*, and contain all the characteristic events.

Gazal. Beautiful verses of *Urdu* and *Persian* poets, set to simple pretty music with simple *Tāla*.

Dhun are fascinating short melodies and mixtures of simple *Rāgas* like *Lavnis*.

Guzzal, *Thumri*, *Dhun*, and such light songs are popular and sung by the high and low. But *Dhrupad* and *Dhamar*, *Sadra*, *Koul*, *Chatrang* and like methods are restricted to some *ustads*. There are some good *Khyal* singers. These styles are difficult, therefore not popular and understood by the masses.

Apart from these methods there are also other ways of singing songs at different occasions. The varied parts of the country have their own individual characteristic singing like *Lachchi* in Punjab, *Mand* in Rajputana. These are evening tunes sung by a maiden who goes to fetch water from a well or by a mother rocking a baby to sleep. They are very beautiful. *Garbās* are gay joyous tunes sung in *Gujerat* and *Kathiawar* on some festive occasions by a group of young maidens. They move in a circular form with slow rhythmic movements, bending their lithe figures gracefully beating their hands in rhythm.

HARMONIOUS AND INHARMONIOUS NOTES IN A TUNE

Badi, *Sambadi*, *Ambadi*, *Bebadi* : these are the four expressions given to the notes which are harmonious or discordant in a tune, for instance :

(1) Badi ; this term is applied to that note which is dominant and gives colour to a tune, like the note *Dha* in the *Rāga Bhairon* ; or the note *Ma* in the *Rāga Malkaus* ; or *Komal Gandhar* (flat *Ga*) in the *Rāginī* (feminine tune) *Todi*.

(2) Sambadi, is the expression which is applied to that note which gives additional brilliance to a tune, and helps the *Badi*, like the *Sur Dha* in *Todi*. This note is sub-dominant.

(3) Ambadi, is the expression applied to those notes which are not discordant in tune.

(4) Bebadi, is the expression applied to a note or notes which are completely discordant in a tune, like *Tivra Ma*, in *Malkaus* ; or *Tivra Ga* in *Todi*.

EXPRESSIONS DENOTING INFORMATION ABOUT RĀGAS AND RĀGINĪS

The following are certain musical expressions used in giving information about the *Rāga* and *Rāginīs*.

Mārg, is the expression applied to those *Rāgas* and *Rāginīs* that are sung exactly alike in all parts of the country, but that the mode of execution should be so difficult, so as not to be comprehensible to all, like the *Khandari-Bani* or *Dhrupad* singing. *Mārg* is celestial.

Desi, is the expression used for those tunes which are sung differently everywhere, but that the method of its singing should be so facile, so as to be understood by all. *Desi* is terrestrial.

Sudha, is the expression given to those tunes which have retained the notes of original purity, untempered by any freak of time or man, like the six *Rāgas* (male tunes), and a few important *Rāginīs* (feminine tunes).

Salink, are those tunes which have semblance of other tunes. These are many.

Sanke-Run are those tunes which are either created out of the combination of two *Shudha* tunes, or five or six *Rāginīs*. These are numerous.

Maha-Salink are those tunes which are formed from *Salink* and *Sanke-Run*. There are no end of these. Some are of a remarkably beautiful and classical nature.

MURCHANA

Murchana is that alluring and pleasing oddity in Indian music which helps to establish the indefinable charm and the merging of tones which characterize the melodies so forcibly and fully.

Murchana is the harmonious and gentle gliding of sounds which occur while uniting one note to the other consecutive one.

There are twenty-one *Murchanas* in the three *Saptaks* (octaves), each *Murchana* comprises the sounds created during the blending of one note into the other of the *Rohi* (ascending from the lower notes to the higher in the scale of one octave), and the *Arohi* (descending from the higher notes to the lower).

The following are the *Murchanas* of the *Mandra Saptak* : (1) *Utra-Manda*, this *Murchana* is formed by starting from the note *Sa*, in the *Rohi* scale, and coming back to the note *Sa*, in the *Arohi* scale. The following *Murchanas* are in their proper order, each having a successive note for a starting-point, in the scale, and coming back to the same point. (2) *Ranjani*. (3) *Utra-tha*. (4) *Suddha-Kharja*. (5) *Bajhri-Karta*. (6) *Ason-Kranta*. (7) *Aph-Rokta*.

Murchanas of the *Madhyam Saptak :* (1) *Sobray*. (2) *Harnsuad*. (3) *Klohna*. (4) *Barkav*. (5) *Parkharka*. (6) *Saddhya*. (7) *Gorpay*.

Murchanas of the *Tar-Saptak :* (1) *Pra*. (2) *Basala*. (3) *Sonky*. (4) *Partarka*. (5) *Roni*. (6) *Barkhata*. (7) *Onta*.

QUALIFICATIONS OF MUSICIANS

In ancient days there were institutions of music where a student acquired knowledge and attained a certain degree of proficiency which qualified him in his profession and gave him a certain standing and position in the musical world. And there is a veritable vocabulary of titles that marked the different grades to which he belonged. I shall quote a few important ones.

Naik was the highest degree conferred on one who was a past-master in the science ; he not only rendered all the *Rāgas* and *Rāginīs* in their original purity and correctness, but was also able to produce pupils equally great. *Baijoo* and *Gopal* were *Naiks*.

Gandharb was the degree given to an efficient performer of *Mārg* an *Dési*. *Tan-Sén* was a *Gandharb*.

Guni was the degree given to him who was able to execute *Dési* well

Pandit was he who learnt the science to perfection in theory but not in practice.

Uttam was the name given to him who had such an extraordinary command over his singing that he could sing without any accompaniment, and not be dependent in any way on his instruments for *Tāla* (time) and *Sur* (note). This is quite extraordinary in the Indian music, and only an efficient student could aspire to attain this rank.

Madhyam was one who was more or less dependent upon his accompaniment.

Adham was he who was entirely dependent upon his accompaniment for singing.

QUALITIES OF VOICE

The singer had to be distinguished with the thirteen qualities in his voice.

Mirisht, that the voice should affect all who heard it.

Madhur, that the voice should be sweet and entertaining.

Jhapal, that the voice should neither be very loud nor very low, but deep and rich, and that while singing he should be able to retain the breath for a long time and not suffer from short breath.

Taras-than. The three *saptaks* should be executed with equal facility and ease.

Sakhaba, that the voice should be possessed of the power of creating laughter in the assembly.

Karan, that the voice should be possessed of such pathos as to produce deep feelings and tears.

Komal, that the voice should be soft and stirring.

Sara-dak, that the voice should be big and heard distinctly at a distance.

Ghan, that the voice should be clear without tremor.

Sang-da, to execute all the *Tans* (variations) with great ease.

Gād, that the command should be so entire as to be able to produce loud and soft sounds at will.

RĀGA MALKAUS

Facing page 68.

Salohan, to be able to sing at length without break.

Parjar, that the singer should be of a prepossessing appearance and noble disposition.

DEFECTS OF MUSICIANS

There were several objectionable mannerisms which disqualified a singer. A long list of them is given in the sacred books. The following are a few :

Sandasht, to sing with closed teeth.

Bhut, to sing with fear.

Sanket, to sing without confidence.

Kāmpat, to start with a tremor in the voice.

Karagi, to sing with mouth wide open.

Kapal, to sing with flourishes.

Kagay, to start with commotion and noise.

Karaba, to crane the neck like a camel.

Jumbuk, to shake and whirl the head and neck while singing.

Parsari, to make frantic gestures with the hands.

Namiluk, to sing with eyes closed tight.

Abagpat, to sing with all the words jumbled up together, and rolling in the throat so as to be incomprehensible.

Stekari, to sing by taking sharp quick breaths.

San-Nasik, to sing with a nasal twang.

Pava-Chat, that the voice should be shaky.

Ase-that, that the voice should be disturbed.

Nasar, that the voice should be closed and tight.

Kaga, that the voice should be like the cawing of a crow.

Karish, that the voice should be thin-flat.

Bhikan, that the voice should resemble the braying of a donkey.

An efficient singer was supposed to follow these and several other injunctions, he was also carefully instructed to impress upon the hearers with the *sum* of the song.

Sum is the important beat or juncture of a tune where all the attention of the hearers is deeply concentrated. In other words it is the climax of the song.

The singer should also be discriminate, and mark the occasion by singing opportune songs. He should have a good memory, and should be something of a poet.

The musician of old days must have been an ideal personage. He was regulated by all the laws so appropriately and becomingly laid down for a master of such an agreeable art.

The modern musician is altogether devoid of these pleasing qualifications, his studies in etiquette of singing neglected and ignored, and that is the reason why modern singing results in grimaces, painful gestures and disagreeable sounds.

TĀNS

A *Tān* is a variation or run, which occurs when a tune is played or sung. There are countless varieties of executing *Tāns*, and these are so numerous that a finished performer can sing or play a tune for hours with the introduction of *Tāns* before he has exhausted his stock, and yet not repeat the same *Tān* twice.

This is that extraordinary part of the Indian music when a musician has the unique opportunity and advantage of asserting his knowledge and individuality during the course of a performance by harmonious combination of notes into *Tāns*—on the spur of the moment.

These *Tāns* are best understood when sung or played : to convey any definite idea of what they really mean in writing is an impossibility.

The inflections, modulations, trill, etc., they form are so numberless and so inspiring that in spite of oneself, one is uplifted in an enchanted region, full of mysterious charms and beauties.

As I have said before, there are various classes of *Tāns*. I shall now endeavour to demonstrate one kind of *Tān* only which produces five thousand and forty ; diversified *Tāns* from the seven notes of the octaves, *Sa*, *Re*, *Ga*, *Ma*, *Pa*, *Dha*, *Ni*.

It may help to convey to the reader the extent of the grandeur and beauties that these tunes possess. It may seem impossible at first glance that such a small number of notes should be able to produce varied strains of

Rāginī Lalit

Facing page 70.

RĀGINĪ GOJRI

such magnitude, but a close study will show how skilfully and with what knowledge it was manipulated by the ancient masters of Indian music.

One note will give you one *Tāna* only, *Sa*. Two notes will give you two *Tāns* of different varieties, *Rohi* (ascending from low to the high notes). (1) *Sa*, *Re*, *Arohi* (descending from the high to the low notes). (2) *Re*, *Sa*. In three notes, *Sa*, *Re*, *Ga*, you get six different *Tāns* : (1) *Sa*, *Re*, *Ga*. (2) *Re*, *Sa*, *Ga*. (3) *Sa*, *Ga*, *Re*. (4) *Re*, *Ga*, *Sa*. (5) *Ga*, *Re*, *Sa*, and (6) *Ga*, *Sa*; *Re*.

Four notes produce twenty-four *Tāns*, thus :

(1) *Sa*, *Re*, *Ga*, *Ma*. (2) *Sa*, *Re*, *Ma*, *Ga*. (3) *Sa*, *Ga*, *Ma*, *Re*. (4) *Sa*, *Ga*, *Re*, *Ma*. (5) *Sa*, *Ma*, *Re*, *Ga*. (6) *Sa*, *Ma*, *Ga*, *Re*.

(7) *Re*, *Ga*, *Ma*, *Sa*. (8) *Re*, *Ga*, *Sa*, *Ma*. (9) *Re*, *Ma*, *Sa*, *Ga*. (10) *Re*, *Ma*, *Ga*, *Sa*. (11) *Re*, *Sa*, *Ga*, *Ma*. (12) *Re*, *Sa*, *Ma*, *Ga*.

(13) *Ga*, *Ma*, *Sa*, *Re*. (14) *Ga*, *Ma*, *Re*, *Sa*. (15) *Ga*, *Sa*, *Re*, *Ma*. (16) *Ga*, *Sa*, *Ma*, *Re*. (17) *Ga*, *Re*, *Sa*, *Ma*. (18) *Ga*, *Re*, *Ma*, *Sa*.

(19) *Ma*, *Ga*, *Re*, *Sa*. (20) *Ma*, *Ga*, *Sa*, *Re*. (21) *Ma*, *Re*, *Ga*, *Sa*. (22) *Ma*, *Re*, *Sa*, *Ga*. (23) *Ma*, *Sa*, *Re*, *Ga*. (24) *Ma*, *Sa*, *Ga*, *Re*.

Five notes have a capacity to create one hundred and twenty *Tāns*.

If the arrangement of the four notes permitting twenty-four *Tans* above, is followed carefully, it will be seen that five notes must needs necessarily furnish one hundred and twenty *Tāns*.

It is clear that four notes produce twenty-four *Tāns*. It is in itself a group of four notes only. Five notes therefore have five groupings of four notes, thus :

Sa, *Re*, *Ga*, *Ma*, *Pa*, are the five notes and in these the five groups of four notes are (1) *Sa*, *Re*, *Ga*, *Ma*. (2) *Re*, *Ga*, *Ma*, *Pa*. (3) *Ga*, *Ma*, *Pa*, *Sa*. (4) *Ma*, *Pa*, *Sa*, *Re*. (5) *Pa*, *Sa*, *Re*, *Ga*, place the remaining note at the beginning of a *Tān*. Each of these groups of four notes will produce twenty-four *Tans*, making in all one hundred and twenty *Tāns*, for example :

Sa (at the beginning of *Tān*), and the remaining four Notes are *Re*, *Ga*, *Ma*, *Pa*.

These four notes will supply twenty-four *Tans* according to the explanation above, thus : (1) *Sa*, *Re*, *Ga*, *Ma*, *Pa*. (2) *Sa*, *Re*, *Ga*, *Pa*, *Ma*. (3) *Sa*, *Ma*, *Pa*, *Ga*, *Re*. (4) *Sa*, *Re*, *Ma*, *Ga*, *Pa*, etc., etc.

When these twenty-four *Tāns* of the hundred and twenty are exhausted, start by placing the consecutive note *Re*, at the commencement of a *Tān*, making a scale like this : *Re*, *Ga*, *Ma*, *Pa*, *Sa—Re* at the beginning and the four notes *Ga*, *Ma*, *Pa*, *Sa*, will yield 24 *Tāns*. Example : *Re*, *Ga*, *Ma*, *Pa*, *Sa*. *Re*, *Ga*, *Ma*, *Sa*, *Pa*. *Re*, *Ga*, *Pa*, *Ma*, *Sa*. *Re*, *Ga*, *Pa*, *Sa*, *Ma*, etc., etc.

Then place the following note at the beginning of a *Tān* and the remaining four notes *Pa*, *Sa*, *Re*, *Ga*, will give twenty-four *Tāns* ; similarly start the *Tāns* with *Pa* and the four notes *Sa*, *Re*, *Ga*, *Ma*, will contain twenty-four *Tāns*, completing the hundred and twenty *Tāns*.

Six notes, *Sa*, *Re*, *Ga*, *Ma*, *Pa*, *Dha*, at once multiply the number of one hundred and twenty *Tāns* six times, making an enormous increase of seven hundred and twenty *Tāns*.

The same method follows the building up of these *Tāns* all throughout, facilitating their comprehension.

The scale of these six notes has six varied groupings of five notes each, with the one extra note which falls at the beginning of each *Tān* successively, as follows :

(1) *Sa*, *Re*, *Ga*, *Ma*, *Pa*. (2) *Re*, *Ga*, *Ma*, *Pa*, *Dha*. (3) *Ga*, *Ma*, *Pa*, *Dha*, *Sa*.
(4) *Ma*, *Pa*, *Dha*, *Sa*, *Re*. (5) *Pa*, *Dha*, *Sa*, *Re*, *Ga*. (6) *Dha*, *Sa*, *Re*, *Ga*, *Ma*.
Each of these groups of five notes forms one hundred and twenty *Tāns*.

Similarly, seven notes form five thousand and forty different *Tāns*. Multiplying the last number of seven hundred and twenty *Tāns*, seven times, making five thousand and forty *Tāns*.

In these seven notes, *Sa*, *Re*, *Ga*, *Ma*, *Pa*, *Dha*, *Ni*, there are seven different groups of six notes :

(1) *Sa*, *Re*, *Ga*, *Ma*, *Pa*, *Dha*. (2) *Re*, *Ga*, *Ma*, *Pa*, *Dha*, *Ni*.
(3) *Ga*, *Ma*, *Pa*, *Dha*, *Ni*, *Sa*. (4) *Ma*, *Pa*, *Dha*, *Ni*, *Sa*, *Re*.
(5) *Pa*, *Dha*, *Ni*, *Sa*, *Re*, *Ga*. (6) *Dha*, *Ni*, *Sa*, *Re*, *Ga*, *Ma*.
With the one note extra, coming at the beginning of the scale of these six notes successively in the order of the octave Each of these groups of six notes yields seven hundred and twenty *Tāns*, and seven hundred and twenty times multiplied by seven, is five thousand and forty *Tāns*.

The skeleton of a *Rāga* or *Rāginī* is sung first, then a line is taken, and

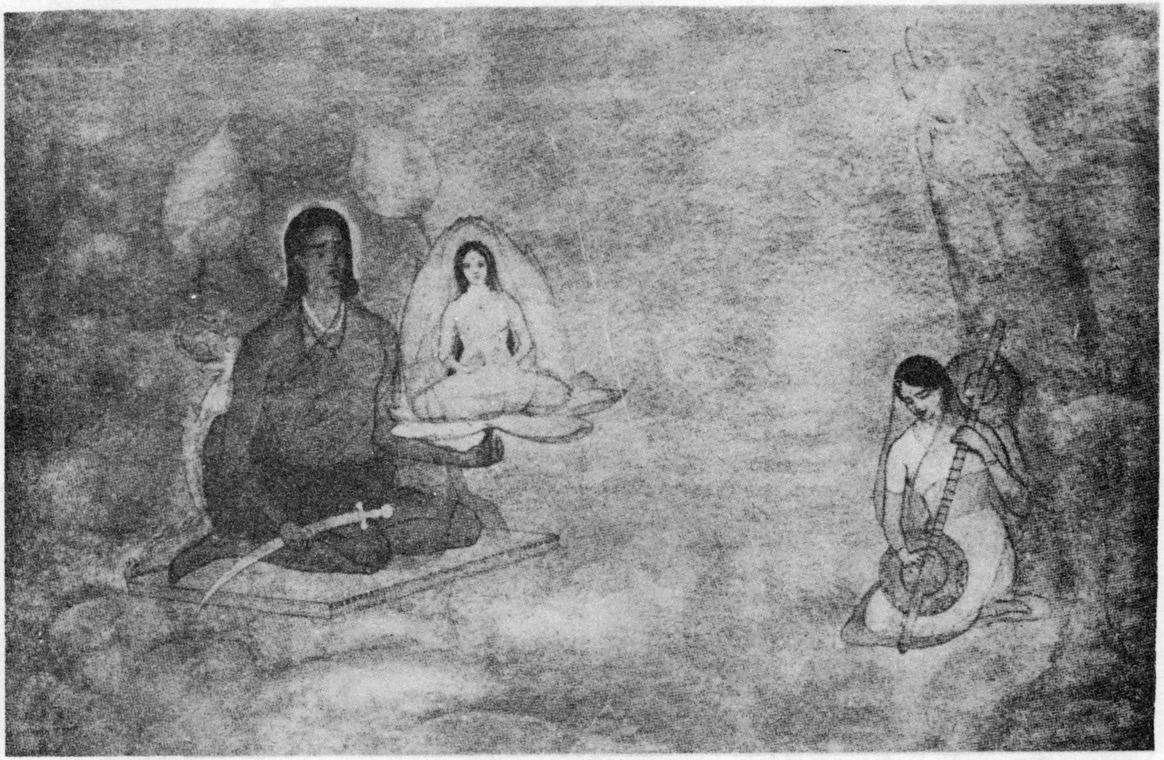

THE MRDANGA

repeated with the introduction of these *Tāns*, and other kinds of *Tāns* which I have not mentioned, but always bearing in mind the scale of the *Rāga* and *Rāginīs* that is sung.

For all the *Rāgas* and *Rāginīs* have their own scales of variegated notes. These *Tans* are adjusted to the scale which is true for that particular *Rāga* which is sung or played. These are called *Kut-Tāns*.

Tāns (expansion) other than above combination of notes by which the melody expands.

Alankar Baran, or *Paltaen*, according to *Parijat*, there are sixty-three varieties, for example :

(1) Bhader — *sr*, *srg*, *rgm*, etc.
(2) Nand — *ss*, *rr*, *gg*, etc.
(3) Jit — *srgs*, *r*, *mgr*, etc.

Kan, to render a higher or lower note—to a *sar* with a slight rapid jerk.

Mend or soot, to slide from *Sur* to *Sur* :

like *S R G M*.

Andolit. Tremor.

Gamak. Pronounced jerk of notes and others.

RĀGAS AND RĀGINĪS

All the *Rāgas*, *Rāginīs*, *Putras* and *Bhāryas*, and other tunes have names to distinguish them from each other, so that there is no confusion. Some are named after deities, some after tribes, some after the composers, some after the countries, etc. They have also appointed seasons of the year and hours of the day, when they should be sung and played. Musicians abide by this law strictly. It may be thought, perhaps, it is merely a matter of imagination and habit of centuries, that a cultivated ear cannot tolerate a song sung out of season or time.

A *Bihag* is full of sweet meanings and appealing sentiments when sung at night ; in the morning it is entirely discordant and loses its beauty. Similarly, an *Asa-ori* sung in the early hours of the day stirs the depths of your higher thoughts ; at night it loses its charm and falls flat.

This is not a matter of habit or imagination ; a deeper mystery pervades the arrangements. There are certain notes that are characterized by fiery temperaments. These are dominant in the tunes to be played or sung in the hot months. Then there are other notes that are attributed with cold temperaments. These are important in the tunes to be played in the cold season.

The musicians of olden days were profound students of nature and knew the cosmic laws. They unravelled the hidden secrets of sound by long study and made sure that certain sounds harmonized with certain notes in certain seasons, and adjusted the notes in accordance with nature.

* The twenty-four hours of a night and day are divided into eight parts, and each part lasts for three hours. The first morning part is from six o'clock to nine o'clock. The tunes that are to be played or sung during these hours are slow, dreamy and pure, and the notes *Re* and *Dha* are *komal* (flat). *Bhairon*, and all its species which are eight, and *Ramkali*, are sung at this time. *Re*, *Ma*, *Dha*, are *komal*.

Nine to twelve is the second morning part. And all the notes that occur in the tunes to be sung and played in these hours are *komal*—like *Asaori-Bhairveen* and *Todi*, and such others. The *Komal* notes now change into *Tivra*. At noon exactly *Sarang* is played. It is a bright melody. All the notes in the *rohi* are *tivra* and *Ma* and *Ni* are *komal* in the *rohi*. *Sarang* is *Udhao*, and has five notes in the scale, viz., *Sa*, *Re*, *Ma*, *Pa*, *Ni*.

From twelve to three, *Bhimpalasi*, *Dhanasari*, *Dhani*, etc., are played. *Ga*, *Ma* and *Ni* in these tunes are *komal* and *Re*, *Dha* that were *komal* in the morning tunes become *Tivra*. Three to six p.m., *Poorvi Purya-dhanasari* and *Marwa* are played in these hours. *Shri Rāga* is played at about six o'clock. *Ga*, *Ma* and *Ni* in these tunes become *Tivra* and *Re* and *Dha* become *Komal*.

From six to nine all the notes become *Tivra*. *Yemen*, *Kalian* and all the *Kalian* tunes—which are numerous—are played in these hours.

From nine to twelve p.m. are played *Bihag-Sankra Desh*, etc. They are all in *Tivra* notes. At about midnight, *Bageshari*, *Behar*, *Adana* and such others, are played ; and *Ga*, *Ma* and *Ni* again become *Komal* in these tunes.

From twelve to three a.m. all kinds of *Kanhras*, which are eighteen in number, are played, including the famous *Durbari* ; excepting *Sugrai Kanhra*, which is played in the morning. *Malkaus* is also played after midnight. The

* **See Appendix, No. II.**

RĀGINĪ ASAORI

Facing page 76.

notes *Re* and *Pa* do not occur in these tunes. All the rest are *Komal.* From three to six a.m. are played *Hindolo*, *Sohni*, *Paraj*, etc. The *Komal* notes of *Malkaus* change into *Tivra* and it becomes *Hindolo*, which is *Odhao.* Then by adding *Re komal*, the tune becomes *Sohni*, which is *Sadhao* ; and then by adding *Pa* to the scale it becomes *Paraj*, *Basant* and *Lalit* are also played in these hours ; both the *Tivra* and the *Komal Ma* occur in these tunes.

Sandhi Prakash. All those melodies which are to be sung at the twilights when a change in nature seems to take place, and they take *Re* and *Dha Komal* and *Ga* and *Ni Tivar*, as in *Bhairaon.*

Tivar Madhyam *Rāgas* are those which are sung in the evening and night.

Shuddh Madhyam *Rāgas* are those which are sung in the morning and day.

The scale is divided into two parts. *Purva Ang* is the first part comprising of *s r g m.*

The *Rāgas* which are recognized by the lower notes *s r g m* of the scale and called *Purva Ang Rāgas* are sung from noon to midnight.

Utter Ang is the second part comprising of *Pans.* The *Rāgas* which are recognized by the higher notes, p d n s of the scale are called *Utter Anga Rāgas.*

These are the valuable observations made by *Pandit Bhatkhande* and facilitate the location of a tune to the hour.

When the *Rāgas* are sung in proper time and season and with perfect knowledge of the science, an absolute and inexpressible sense of calm and inner satisfaction is derived.

In such a state of perfection the *Rāgas* are supposed to be possessed of supernatural powers.

They have chronicles of their births, which point out the mysterious sources from which they have originated. They have a series of interesting legends, recording their life-histories. They are benefactors of humanity, by curing various bodily ailments. They charm the elements of nature and invoke fire and water ; in short, they perform miracles.

The idea of personifying all the forces of Nature seems to be quite common in Hinduism. All the *Rāgas* and *Rāginīs* are impersonated. There are quatrains and verses illustrating the form, colour, symbolism and meanings of each tune. The *Rāgas* and *Rāginīs* have been favourite themes with old Indian artists, who have painted them over and over again, but a fine illustration is rarely seen nowadays.

CHRONICLES OF RĀGAS AND RĀGINĪS

Mahadev, the god of music, is distinguished by having five heads. Each of the four heads being turned towards the four quarters of the globe, north, south, east and west, while the fifth head is turned towards the Heavens. And from each of the five heads the five great *Rāgas* or demi-gods, *Bhairon*, *Hindole*, *Dipak*, *Shri* and *Megh* originate. The sixth *Rāga*, *Malkus*, comes out of *Parvati*, the wife of *Mahadev*. *Brahma* created the thirty *Rāginīs* or nymphs, and each *Rāga* or demi-god was presented with five *Rāginīs* of sympathetic strains, whom he preserved with the tenderest care. *Saraswati*, the goddess of Music and Learning and the wife of *Brahma*, left an exquisitely graceful and poetic legacy to the world, in the shape of *Vina*, the most cherished and valued musical instrument in India and the demi-god *Narada* was appointed to play it.

"From *Nada* (sound) arose *Surti*.
From *Surti* came *Swara* (tone).
And from *Swara* was formed *Rāga* (scale).
And from *Rāga* was created *Gita* (tune).
So that the soul of *Gita* is sound."

Rāga means passions, and different tunes excite different emotions and feelings, such as *Bhairveen*, is significant of beauty. *Nut*, of valour. *Marwa*, of fear. *Shri*, of grandeur, *Malkaus*, of passion, *Asaori*, of renunciation, *Bihag* of joy and brightness.

Rāga-Bhairon. This *Rāga* originates from that head of *Mahadev* which is turned southwards. This tune along with its *Rāginīs*, *Putras* and *Bharyas*, may be played in the months of September and October. The time for its performance is from early dawn to sunrise. It is *sumpooran*, i.e., has all the seven notes of the octave for its scale. *Sa*, *Re* (*komal*), *Ga*, *Ma*,

RĀGINĪ BHAIRVEEN

Facing page 78.

Pa, *Dha* (*komal*), *Ni* ; in the *Rohi* and *Arohi*. In form it is like *Mahadev*, having five heads, four heads turned towards the four directions—north, south, east and west—while the fifth head is turned towards the Heavens. He is represented as a *Yogi* or *Sanyasi* (one who has retired from the world). His body is besmeared with ashes, his tresses, grey with dust, are gathered on the top of the head ; two *Gangas* (rivers) come out from his hair and flow on either side of his head. These are the two sacred rivers in India, the *Ganga* and the *Yumna*. A jewelled *Kangan* (bracelet) is fastened on his wrist, and a crescent in the centre of the head. The third eye of wisdom is located between the eyebrows. Two powerful *Cobras* (Cobra de Capello) are coiled round his arms, on the forehead is the mark of the sacred emblem, called the *Thripunda*. He is seated on a skin of tiger in the heavens, encircled by glittering clouds, holding a trident in one hand, and a rosary of *Rudrakhas* in the other. His throat is adorned with a chaplet of eight human skulls.

Bhairon has five *Rāginīs* : *Berari*, *Madhmad*, *Bhairveen*, *Sindhavi* and *Bengal*. The *Rāginīs* are represented as ideal graces of womanhood, most divinely fair and of incomparable beauty. The radiance they shed is so great that the sun seems as if ashamed, who hides his face behind the clouds, and the moon withdraws in modest retirement on seeing their sweet lustre.

The description of the *Rāginī Bhairveen*, is sylph-like and of a most exquisite symmetry, with the youthful freshness and bloom of a shy young maiden of seventeen. Her hair still humid with the *Snāna* (sacred bath) is thrown back in a heavy dark mass. From beneath her long drooping eye-lashes, there escapes an ineffable light, giving a calm serenity to the beautiful profile. Her slim hands are clasped in reverence. Her whole attitude is bent in submissive religious fervour. A breathing poem of devotion at the altar of the *Ṣiva Linga*. She has taken out her garland, heavily scented of golden *Champas* (flowers) and has consecrated it to the gods.

The scheme of colour of her costume and jewels is red and white. Her dainty person is bejewelled, and enveloped in an opalescent gossamer, more of an imaginary description. The temple of *Mahadev* is built on the summit of a hill encircled by a fort. Flowering blooms of the lotus scent the atmosphere. Two young maidens are engaged in playing and singing on the *Majira* (musical bells). Pearly dawn is creeping invisibly bathing the realm with a delicate

and roseate light. This is the enchanted hour when the tune *Bhairveen* is sung.

The tune is *Sampooran. Sa*, *Re* (*komal*), *Ga* (*komal*), *Ma* (*komal*), *Ma* (*tivra*), *Pa*, *Dha* (*komal*), *Ni* (*komal*) in the *Rohi*. The scale changes in the *Arohi* and only one *Ma* (*tivra*) is retained.

Shri-Rag. It is created out of that head of *Mahadev* which is turned towards the east. This tune along with its female tunes, may be played in the months of November and December. The hour of its performance is about 6 p.m. It is *Sampooran* and has given notes in the octave. *Sa*, *Re* (*komal*), *Ga*, *Ma* (*tivra*), *Pa*, *Dha* (*komal*), *Ni*, in the *Rohi* and *Arohi*.

N.B.—The *Tamboura* (musical instrument), in the hands of the singing girl in the painting, is a mistake on the part of the artist. It should be a *Majira* instead.

In appearance it is like a man dressed in red garments with a handsome pearl and ruby necklace and drops of the same in the ears, holding a sacred lotus flower in his hand, seated on a royal dais, wrapt in listening to the intoxicating strains of the *Vina* (musical instrument), with his lovely companion. "The *Shrirāga* is famous in the Hindu musical realm, sports sweetly with his nymphs, gathering fresh blossoms from the bosom of yon grove and his Divine lineaments are distinguished through his graceful vesture."

Shri-Rāga has five *Rāginīs* : *Basant*, *Malsarī*, *Asaorī*, *Marwā* and *Dhanasrī*. The *Rāginis* are represented as shy young maidens of surpassing loveliness, living in perpetual spring and seeking heavenly bliss in music.

Asaori has an ascetic character. It is represented as a female *Yogin* (one who has renounced the world), seated on a promontory inside a fort, surrounded by water, and beneath a huge *Sandal* tree. Its delicate, massive and perfumed foliage is bent towards her in tender protection and is shading her from the morning sun's warm rays. The hour for its performance is morning. Her dawning womanhood is arrayed in the simple salmon-coloured garb of a *Yogin* (female ascetic), defining the beautiful and subtle lines of her figure. Her raven hair is massed on top of the head. On the white brow gleams the sacred emblem of religion in camphor. Her slumberous eyes are heavy and languorous, with the power of her own music. Her sweet mouth is intent on blowing the soul-stirring notes of the *Pugi* (musical instru-

Rāgiṇī Toḍī

Facing page 80.

ment). Her personality glows with music. The serpents and peacocks are attracted beyond control by her music. They creep and crawl towards her, amazed and entranced.

N.B.—The Sandal-wood tree has a great attraction for serpents, as the flute (*Poongi*) has.

Ràga-Malkaus. This *Rāga* has originated from *Parvati*, the wife of *Mahadev*. The tune with its *Rāginīs*, *Putras* and *Bhāryas* may be sung in January and February, which are the months congenial to these tunes. The hour in which it should be performed is past midnight. It is *Udhao* and has *Sa*, *Ga*, *Ma* and *Ni* notes in the scale. All the notes are *komal*. He is represented as a glorified image of the rich, deep, passionate and mystical melody. Dressed in soft blue, his dreamy eyes are veiled with emotion. He is holding a severed human head in one hand and a naked sword in the other. He stands entranced listening to the delicious music by the maidens, in the undefined distance. Towering on either side are the *Morechals* (insignia of royalty).

N.B.—The idea of conquering enemies is a favourite one in Indian music. The *Rāgas* were qualified as brave, undaunted warriors overcoming their formidable opponents.

Malkaus has five *Rāginīs* : *Jambhavatī*, *Gunkalī*, *Todī*, *Gourī* and *Kaukab*. The *Rāginīs* are fair bevies of beauties, each lovelier than the other, dreaming away the pleasant hours of life in enjoyment and sweet musings. No cares or troubles cross their serene path, no clouds disturb the eternal gay sunshine of their lives.

Todi is represented as a young maiden of ravishing fairness. Dressed in white and gold with the sacred emblem marked in *Camphor* and *Saffron* on her brow. Seated on a hilltop in the midst of a lovely forest, wholly absorbed in playing of the *Vina*. Her pulses beat in a rhythmical whirl of emotion, causing a crimson tinge to rise on her lily-white cheeks. The dark depths of her eyes catch the gold of the rising morning sun. The time for the execution of this tune is morning.

The wild deer venture within the sacred precincts of the temple in meek submission and adoration, completely fascinated and subdued by so glorious a picture and such thrilling music.

N.B.—Certain tunes attract certain animals in nature. The *Todi* is always associated with the deer whom it subjugates.

Rāga Hindol. This *Rāga* has sprung from that mouth of *Mahadev* which is turned towards the north. The months in which it should be played are March and April. The hour for this performance is when the night has far advanced. It is *Udhao*, and has only five notes of the octave in the scale, *Sa*, *Ga*, *Ma*, *Dha*, *Ni*. The latter four notes, *Ga*, *Ma*, *Dha*, *Ni* are *Tivra* in the *Rohi* and *Arohi*.

In form it is like *Krishna*, the god of Love, seated on a *Hindola* (cradle), playing the *Bānsari* (musical instrument), surrounded by his *gopis* who are swinging him in responsive motion of their songs and his *Bānsari*. The liquid depths of his eyes are brimful of mirth and love, locks dark as musk are braided away from his forehead. Rainbow-coloured draperies of gossamer airiness encircle the graceful form of the young maidens, kissing the blooming cheeks and falling lightly over their heads. Jewels shed their brilliant lustre, enhancing the chiselled loveliness of face and figure. *Hindol* has five *Rāginīs* : *Bīlawal*, *Ramkalī*, *Lalitā*, *Dev-Sakh* and *Patman-jari*. The *Rāginīs* live in a nest of swansdown, in their soft sweet thoughts. Their years of musical life roll smoothly by.

Lalita is represented as the most exquisite specimen of feminine beauty. Her skin is lily-white with a lustrous brilliance behind it. Her bejewelled and beautiful head poised on a graceful neck, defies rivalry of the jewelled arms, throat, ears and feet. Golden gauzes of scintillating tints of glorious colours and richness float round her exquisite symmetrical form, disclosing the perfect lines. Her perfumed tresses are thrown in a dense cloud behind. The mysterious expression of her large limpid eyes is partly revealed in the shadow of the long dark, silken lashes which veil them. She reclines with ease on the flower-besprinkled, gorgeous divan, subjugating the senses by her poetic grace and indefinable elegance. A woman with a garland of flowers is standing near her in attendance, gazing on her rapturously.

It is *Sampooran* and both the *Ma* (*komal*) and *Tivra* occur in this tune. The scale differs in the *Rohi* and *Arohi*. *Rohi* : *Sa*, *Re* (*komal*), *Ga*, *Ma* (*komal*), *Ma* (*tivra*), *Dha* (*komal*), *Ni*. *Arohi* : *Sa*, *Ni*, *Dha* (*komal*), *Pa*, *Ma* (*komal*), *Ma* (*tivra*), *Ga* *Re*.

RĀGA DĪPAKA

Facing page 82.

Rāga Dipak. The tune of fire. ***Dipak*** is created out of that mouth of *Mahadev* which is turned towards the east. This tune with its *Rāginīs*, *Putras* and *Bharyas* may be played in the months of May and June, the hottest time of the year. And the hour for its performance is dusk when the shades of the night are beginning to gather on the waning light of the day. This tune has the remarkable power of invoking fire in Nature and if played at the right hour with that correctness which it demands the effect is so magical that all the lights burn instantaneously. It is a very complicated and classical tune. The scale differs in the *Rohi* and *Arohi*. *Rohi* : *Sa*, *Ga*, *Ma* (*tivra*), *Pa*, *Dha* (*komal*), *Pa*, *Sa*. *Arohi* : *Sa*, *Ni*, *Dha* (*komal*), *Ni*, *Sa*, *Ga*, *Pa*, *Ma* (*tivra*), *Ga*, *Re* (*komal*), *Sa*.

This mystic *Rāga* is extinct now and the legend attached to its extirpation is that the Court musician, *Tān Sén*, was singing it in the presence of the mighty Emperor Akbar. His whole soul poured into the piece of music he was singing and note after note vibrated through the air, and thrilled the hearers. His song had no ending, till at last even Nature was moved beyond control. Fire was ignited through the occult power and the *Dipaka Rāga*, and the place was in flames.

This extraordinary incident has proved fatal to the tune, and none has dared to sing it since. The awe and fear with which it is regarded even to-day is beyond belief. The greatest musician will bend his head in reverence and silence at its very name, and will refuse the honour of singing it. It is strange that an incident which happened centuries ago should still exercise the same influence on the minds of the people—as if it had happened to-day.

The notes are there, the melody is there, but no one has the courage and boldness to sing it and the deplorable fact remains that one of the six great *Rāgas* is lost to the world, perhaps for a mere superstition. The tradition goes on to say that the record may only break if the world produces another *Tān Sén*, which is not likely.

Dipak is represented as a handsome young man in the prime of life, most gorgeously robed in red, sparkling in darkness. The brilliancy of his person is so enormous that the rays penetrate the gloom and shoot like tongues of fire.

Dipak has five *Rāginīs : Kamode*, *Desi*, *Kanhra*, *Kidara* and *Nut.*

These female tunes have variegated qualifications. *Kamode* and *Desi* are personifications of " beauties in distress." *Kidara* has lost her individuality in thought of *Mahadev*, and her contemplation of the deity has been so deep that her person has actually assumed the form of the Divinity. She is represented as *Mahadev.*

Nut and *Kanhra* are magnificent women with moral and physical courage :

" Daring and bold in War.

Ardent and impatient in Love."

Nut is represented as a conquering hero having overcome her enemy after a brief struggle and holds a severed head in one hand and a naked sword in the other.

Kanhra has clear-cut handsome features and dignity of manner and personality. She is dressed in white, covered with shimmering gems. Her brow is graced with the sacred emblem of religion in camphor. She holds one tooth of an elephant in one hand and a naked sword in the other. A massive grey elephant is cowering before her, supplicating for his lost tooth. Her delicate nostrils are dilated in disdain. Her dark eyes flash fire. She gives him a withering glance.

There are eighteen varieties of this tune and most of them are *Salinkh*, i.e., having semblance of other tunes.

The time for its performance are the early hours of the night.

Rāga Megh. This has come out of the fifth head of *Mahadev*, which is turned heavenwards. The months in which it should be played are July and August.

It is the Lord of Rains.

It charms the element of water in nature and acts as a spell to bring forth torrents of rain flooding the country. It may be played at all times of the rainy season. *Megh* is represented as a dark, handsome man of formidable appearance. He holds a naked sword in the hand flourishing in mid-air, as if to rend the very skies growling and snarling in rage. He scowls heavily. His eyes are fierce. His hair is drawn upwards and twisted like a turban. The heavens are blackened with angry clouds. Thunder and lightning tear the murky and thick atmosphere, creating an altogether dreadful aspect.

RĀGINĪ KANHRA

Facing page 84.

It is *Sampooran Sa, Ra, Ga, Ma, Pa, Dha, Ni* (*komal*), and *Ni* (*tivra*) in *Rohi* and *Arohi*.

Megh has five *Rāginis : Bhopali, Malar, Gojri, Tunk* and *Deyce-kar*. All are lovely maidens of young years, leading happy lives of unbroken joys and pleasing thoughts.

Gojri is represented as a blushing young maiden dressed in an orange and crimson scarf wound round her beautiful limbs, seated on a flower-besprinkled meadow, engaged in playing and singing on the *been* with her companion.

CHAPTER VIII

Tales of Indian Music

Music has a wonderful power over animals, and certain tunes exercise fascination on certain animals.

(1) Siraj-ud-dowlah used to hold concerts in the jungles for the benefit of the animals, and when *Todi* was played it attracted the deer who would come nearer and nearer listening to the strains with rapture and pleasure. Similarly, *Asaori* would attract serpents and peacocks.

(2) Mirza Mohammad Bulbul would play the *Nai* in his garden. The nightingales would hover around him and flutter from branch to branch until they actually dropped down in a state of ecstasy.

(3) The Prince of Mysore would take his court musicians to a neighbouring district, inhabited by deadly snakes. The performers would form into a circle and play the *Poongi*. As the sounds grew louder, they would draw the snakes from their holes, who came gliding to the place whence the sounds came. They would crawl and creep towards the players encircling them on all sides, rear up their heads, and sway perfectly intoxicated with the weird sounds.

As soon as the music stopped, they would glide away quietly without injuring anyone.

(4) Kidara, the female tune, is connected with a superstitious belief that those who play it come to grief, that is why it is unpopular. It is an extremely classical and pretty air.

(5) Mahadev went to *Naradji* and said, "What do you know of *Vina* playing that you dare to attempt to handle the sacred instrument?" *Naradji* said, "If you can produce anyone who has the courage to play before me I will acknowledge his superiority."

Mahadev at once sent for *Saraswati* and asked her to perform before him.

Naradji was breathless with surprise at her great ability and bowed down before her as the presiding Deity of Music.

(6) Hanuman was very proud of his musical attainments, and foolishly boasted about it. *Rama* was annoyed on hearing this and devised a plan to humble his boastings.

In the jungles there dwelt a noble *Rishi* who practised music with success, until he caused the *Sapt-Swara* (seven notes) to become embodied in seven lovely nymphs.

On the pretext of hunting, *Rama* took *Hanuman* in the vicinity of the abode of the *Rishi*, and begged of him to give them some music. In the meantime, *Hanuman*, wanting to show off his qualifications, took up the *Vina* proudly and began to play.

Just then the seven lovely *nymphs* or notes, passed by them ; they were going to fetch water. Hearing the music one stopped, swayed and fell dead. Hanuman had sung that note incorrectly.

The sister notes (*nymphs*) were comfortless, and moaned and lamented her death piteously : the *Rishi* seeing all smiled, took up the *Vina* and struck the notes loudly. As soon as the dead note (*nymph*) was played correctly it revived and gaily rejoined the sister notes and there was much rejoicing.

Hanuman, thoroughly ashamed of himself, hung his head down and performed penance for his silly vanities.

(7) In the reign of the great Emperor *Akbar* their lived a saint-ascetic, named *Haridas Swami*, in *Muthra*, whose wonderful acquisition of music reached the ears of the Emperor, and he was impatient to behold him. He tried his best to see him and failed. At last he sent for *Tān Sén* and confided in him his troubles. *Tān-Sén* replied : " He is greater than all emperors, O Emperor, and recognizes no man on earth, save his own glorious sacred art which he respects above all. He will not come to see you, but if you condescend to go to *Muthra* you will see him." *Akbar* accordingly travelled to *Muthra*, and beheld the great *Swami* commanding the presence of the *Rāginīs* to appear at will in their own glorious and beautiful form with the power of his tunes.

When *Bhaiveen* came she looked dejected and sad. The Emperor asked her the reason of her sorrow, and she replied, " What can I do ? I am most unhappy. It is this *Tannu* (*Tān-Sén*) who disturbs my peace by playing at all seasons and hours not congenial to me."

Akbar perfectly wonderstruck, recognized the greatness of the *Swami*.

(8) Music flourished considerably under the distinguished patronage of the Moghul Emperors. *Aurangzeb*, the last great Moghul Emperor, was a bigoted Mohammadan and had a caustic dry nature, which checked the flow of all arts, and music specially suffered at his hands. The people got stifled and devised a scheme to soften his hard heart. They prepared a bier, and beating their breasts and tearing their hair, passed it slowly under his window. The solemn and heart-rending sight impressed him. He inquired the reason of their wild grief, and was told that the goddess of Music had died for want of appreciation and was being buried. "Dig the grave deep," he cried, "so that no sound or echo should reach forthwith."

(9) Tān-Sén, the court-musician, the last and greatest singer that India had produced, had such extraordinary power over his music that by way of boasting he began singing one of the night-tunes at noon. He sang with such effect that so far as his glorious voice could reach, the world became enveloped in darkness.

(10) Tān-Sén was once singing *Rāga Dipak* in the court of *Akbar*, and the place was in flames.

A water-carrying maiden passed within its precincts and hearing the tunes and seeing the place in flames stopped, set the vessel down, clasped her hands and bent her figure supplicating the god to assist her, stood up again and drawing a deep breath began to sing *Rāga Megh*. She sang this with such sincerity that the Heavens were disturbed and rain poured forth in torrents, extinguishing the flames.

Skilful performers have often averted famine by singing the *Rāga Megh*.

(11) There are many legends attached to the fiery qualities of the *Rāga Dipak*.

In the innermost sanctuary of an old temple, there burned a sacred light for ages, and through the forgetfulness of the priest to fill it with fresh oil, the light became extinguished. The whole country was at once thrown in disturbance and despair. They attributed the incident to some evil spirit hovering round them, and thought all ills would now befall the country.

A famous musician hearing of this offered to burn the light with the magic power of his song.

The *Rāja* of the land escorted him with great honour to the shrine.

At the hour congenial to the *Rāga* he began his song and sang it with such effect that there gleamed a tiny light in the innermost gloom of the sanctuary. Then, one by one, all the *deevas* (lamps) were mysteriously lighted.

He had averted the calamity.

(12) The end of *Naik Gopal*, one of the mightiest singers the world has produced, was most tragic. Emperor Akbar, in one of his moods, insisted on his singing the *Rāga Dipak*. The celebrated singer had at this stage attained such high perfection that he could not sing a song without stirring the supernatural forces of Nature.

He begged of the Emperor to hold him excused, but the monarch's wayward wishes had to be humoured.

Gopal disappeared for six months and came back prepared to meet his awful doom.

He placed himself neck-deep in the sacred waters of the *Yumna* and began his song. The pure notes vibrated the air. The water began to heat and soon began to boil. The slow torture of the singer was more than he could bear. He begged of the Emperor to allow him to discontinue. *Akbar* was merciless, and the unfortunate singer was compelled to resume the fatal tune.

In the agony of his dreadful sufferings he burst forth with tremendous vigour and sang with such power that the element of fire was excited in Nature, each note turned to flame, and his whole person exhaled fire and slowly consumed his body.

Tān-Sén had four sons, and unlike their father, they had no taste for music. The eldest son, called *Bilas Khan*, was of a roving nature, and inhabited the jungles. It was a great disappointment to the people that none of his own sons were capable of occupying the same high position in the musical world as the great father, and that one of his pupils might have to be selected to take his place after his death.

In course of time *Tān-Sén* died, and the question now arose as to who should be appointed in his place.

The pupils fought among themselves for supremacy. The public could not decide—as one was as good as another. In the meantime, *Bilas Khan* returned from his wanderings, saw his revered father's coffin lying on the threshold, and became very sad; he also saw his dear mother inconsolable, bemoaning the loss of a great name.

He stepped into their midst and said: "He who can move my father's coffin with his song will be awarded the *Pugree* (turban).

The pupils were staggered to hear this bold proposal and stood still and frightened.

When no one answered his challenge he sang the *Rāgini Todi* with such pathos and feeling that the coffin actually moved.

People acknowledged his greatness and the Emperor tied the turban on his head.

The tune is now known as "*Bilas Khani Todi.*" It is a dignified, manly and slow melody.

Al Farabi, the great scholar and philosopher, and inventor of the musical instrument, *Kaanoon*, once went to the Court of *Saifuddowlah*, who was holding a Durbar of learned men.

Al Farabi was in the habit of hiding his identity by donning the uniform of a Turkish soldier.

Saifuddeen, on seeing him, motioned him to sit down. *Farabi* said, "In my place or in yours?"

The king, a little angered, said, "Of course in yours." On hearing this the philosopher pressed his way through the throng, reached the dais and sat down.

Saifuddeen was compelled to move away a little—*Farabi* pressed further until he occupied the central seat. The king, pale with anger, addressed his slaves in a language incomprehensible to most of those present, and said, "I shall put him a few learned questions; if he is able to reply, all well and good, if not you may do away with him. The old fellow is impudent and mannerless, and we shall have to teach him a lesson." The old philosopher immediately replied fluently in the same language, and said, "Have some patience, your Majesty, and await results!" The king was dumfounded, and said, "Do you then understand this language?" *Farabi* said, "Not only this, but

APPENDIX

ASTROLOGICAL SIGNIFICANCE TABLE

BY [illegible] SESSODIA

Svaras	Sanskrit names of the places of origin of the same	English names of the same	Names of the lunar constellations ruling each Svara.[1]	Signs of the Zodiac.	[illegible]	[illegible]
Shadja	Nābhi	Navel	Satabhishja	Kumbha (Aquarius) ♒	Saturn	Positive or Masculine
Rishabha	Hridhaya	Heart	Chitra	Thulā (Libra) ♎	Venus	Positive or Masculine
Gāndhāra	Kanta	Throat	Pushya	Karkata (Cancer) ♋	Moon	Negative or Feminine
Madhyama	Thālu	Palatal	Magha	Simha (Leo) ♌	Sun	Positive or Masculine
Panchama	Nāsika	Nose	Uttra	Kanya (Virgo) ♍	Mercury	Negative or Feminine
Dhaivatam	Danta	Teeth	Purva-Ashada	Dhanus (Sagittarius) ♐	Jupiter	Positive or Masculine
Nishāda	Osh[illegible]	Lips	Anurādh[illegible]	Vrishchica (Scorpio) ♏	Mars	Negative or Feminine

1. In the Swarta-Mahodaya by Nārada the Nakshatra Dhanistha is given as the Nakshatra [illegible] Moon [illegible] the only sign which the Moon rules, I have taken "Pushya" instead.
2. The hours begin from sunrise. The day portion, i.e., from sunrise to sunset is divided into [illegible]
3. Sub-periods are the 15 parts of an astrological hour. In the case of a positive hour [illegible]
4. [illegible] colours could not be given for occult reasons.

seventy more!" He at once rose in the estimation of the king, and there followed a learned discourse, in which all the scholars were defeated.

The king then said, "Now what can I do for you? Will you have some refreshment?" On getting a reply in the negative, he sent for all his court musicians of renown, and they began to perform. *Farabi* criticized the knowledge and performance of each, until the king got disgusted, and said, "Perhaps you yourself can perform better." *Farabi* quietly took out a few pieces of reeds from his pocket, adjusted them, and began to play a bright melody. The result was that the whole company burst into an incontrolable fit of mirth. He then changed his tune and began to play mournful notes, with such effect that all present were moved to tears. Again he changed his theme, playing slowly and dreamily, until gradually the listeners sank into a profound slumber, when he quietly slipped away.

APPENDIX I

BY

Thakur Sri Jessrājsinghji Seesodia of Udaipur

ASTROLOGY

Innumerable references to planetary rulerships, temperaments, colours, seasons, periods and other astrological matters by the *Begum Sahibā*, without any explanation, have made it obligatory to add a few appendices on the subjects unexplained, instead of foot-notes as was originally intended.

This is the first instance in which the connection of astrology with music has been referred to by an author writing in English on Indian music. The works on music in Sanskrit, Persian, or the other vernaculars of India, devote a section on the connection of music to astrology; but no recent author, European or Indian, who has written in English on Indian music, has ever touched the subject in connection with music.

This may be partly owing to ignorance of the subject, and partly to popular prejudice, but in any case as the *Begum Sahibā* has touched upon the subject which is the very key to music from an Indian point of view, it has become necessary to explain the *rationale* of astrology in connection with music. The connection of astrology with music in general, and with Indian music in particular, is highly interesting as it explains a certain phenomenon hitherto unexplained in Western music, and it is very important from an occult point of view to understand the *raison d'être* of it. Music in India is part of the occult science, hence the rigid rules and canons regarding its instrumental execution or vocal demonstration in keeping to certain times, seasons, days and hours, which are strictly adhered to by the great master musicians of the country.

In India, to music is attributed extraordinary potentialities of phenomena-producing properties. Whether this is justified or not is only to be judged by thoroughly going into the matter in all its phases, as required by the canons of astrology. Indian musicians, when requested to prove the marvellous powers attributed to the *Rāga-Rāginīs*, one and all give the same answer, that is, that one could not properly judge a musical demonstration of the above description, unless it was given under correct astrological conditions. Hence this appendix to explain the *rationale* of astrology to European and American readers, who are unacquainted with the subject, so that they may verify the facts mentioned in the book, if desired.

Astrology, as known to the West, is still in its infancy, as it is only applied to some phases of life, but not known as the basis of cosmic law, though it may have been better known in ages past. Owing to popular prejudice and religious opposition, it has been very much kept in the background, hence its full development and growth has been greatly hindered, and owing to this attitude many pretenders to this sublime science, without any special training or knowledge, have come into existence. The science of astrology in India is studied under rigid conditions and by people of very high academical attainments. One has to be a good mathematician and astronomer to become a good astrologer in India.

It is curious that such eminent astrologers and men of science and philosophy as Newton and Bacon in England, and Kepler and Tycho Brahe on the Continent, who were all ardent astrologers as well as being prominent men in their own spheres of science, as they knew it to be the only key to cosmic forces, should have their opinions regarding astrology ignored by their own countrymen. This has made it possible for charlatans to dupe people in the name of this most occult science, owing to its non-patronage by men of science—by non-patronage I mean men of scientific attainments not taking up the study seriously to investigate the truth of it ; as a thorough knowledge of real astrology is hard to be achieved without possessing the required attainments from an Indian point of view. By the above remarks I do not mean that sham astrology does not exist in India. On the contrary, it also flourishes there and caters to the silly and the simple as in Europe, but in its higher adherents, it has men of culture and position who devote years to its study, and owing to its hidden symbology as an occult key to all cosmic laws it is very difficult to acquire. It is only through this key that the cosmic secrets can be made known to man, and the reason of its application to this highly cultivated science of music. Music in India or to the Hindu is a part of the divine revelation, therefore is held in high veneration. Let it not be misunderstood when we say divine ***revelation***, that it is meant in the sense that Christianity understands the word revelation, but as having been taught by men who had reached, through self-abnegation, higher states, so as to have developed higher mentalities to see or rediscover the eternal truth which is hidden to the ignorant and known to the wise. In that sense it is a part of the *Gāndharva Veda*, one of the *Upa Vedas* of the Hindus.

The marvellous wonder-working phenomena of Indian music can only be achieved by the knowledge of the cosmic laws through the key of astrology. No one would regard as a miracle the raising of a wheat crop by a farmer, who is guided solely by natural laws, which he has learned by watching and tabulating, instead of sowing in mid-winter, waits till spring, and achieves it. It is only by synchronizing the natural laws to his own knowledge, and this is due to past experience. The science of agriculture is entirely guided by the tabulated experience of past generations, codified and reduced to a precise science.

So, music, when made to synchronize with certain seasons, days, hours, and sub-periods, also conforms to cosmic laws and produces effects when desired, and is thus workable according to the canons of astrology, if properly adhered to and rigidly followed.

The *Begum Sahibā* refers to the seven planets in connection with the seven *surs* (*svarās*), and emphasizes the fact that it is very necessary, if phenomenon is desired in playing or singing the *Rāga-Rāginīs*, that particular attention must be paid to time, that is, in reference to special days, hours, months, seasons, etc.

The canons of starology attribute certain elemental properties to the seven planets, and as these seven planets are also given rulerships of the twelve signs of the zodiac, each of the four gross elements, air, fire, water and earth, or in other words, *soniferous*, *gaseous*, *liquid*, and *solid*, has a group of three signs of the zodiac assigned to one of the elements. Hence the statement about the *Dipak Rāga*, that when it is played or sung it produces heat or flames, is owing to its hot temperament, and this only if properly sung or played at the precise moment on the exact day synchronizing with the season and the place, by a fit person whose knowledge is perfect in the science of music, and so on with each of the *Rāga-Rāginīs*.

A special Table made to show the relationship is given for the benefit of readers, with a comprehensive description, with tables to calculate time at different latitudes, and the way to synchronize the elements with the *Rāga-Rāginīs*, and the various methods of manipulation to produce effect.